Management Accounting

SAGE COURSE COMPANIONS
KNOWLEDGE AND SKILLS *for* SUCCESS

Management Accounting

Alicia Gazely and
Michael Lambert

SAGE Publications

London ● Thousand Oaks ● New Delhi

First published 2006

SAGE Publications Ltd
1 Oliver's Yard
55 City Road
London EC1Y 1SP

SAGE Publications Inc.
2455 Teller Road
Thousand Oaks, California 91320

SAGE Publications India Pvt Ltd
B-42, Panchsheel Enclave
Post Box 4109
New Delhi 110 017

British Library Cataloguing in Publication data

A catalogue record for this book is available from
the British Library

ISBN-10 1-4129-1884-7 ISBN-13 978-1-4129-1884-8
ISBN-10 1-4129-1885-5 ISBN-13 978-1-4129-1885-5 (pbk)

Library of Congress Control Number: 2005934168

Typeset by C&M Digitals (P) Ltd., Chennai, India
Printed in Great Britain by The Cromwell Press Ltd, Trowbridge, Wiltshire
Printed on paper from sustainable resources

contents

This SAGE Course Companion offers you a guide to making the most of your studies in management accounting. Ideally, you should buy this book at the beginning of your course and use it throughout your studies to help you to understand basic ideas and fit new ideas into an overall framework. Whichever way you use it, it will provide you with essential help with revising for your course exams, preparing and writing course assessment materials, and enhancing and progressing your knowledge and thinking skills in line with course requirements.

This book should be seen as a supplement to your textbook and lecture notes. It isn't intended to replace your textbooks or lectures – it is intended to save you time when you are revising for your exams or preparing coursework. Note that RE-vision implies that you looked at the subject the first time round!

Whichever textbook you are using, the basics are the basics: we have given some guidance on where topics are covered in specific books, but you should read the Companion in parallel with your textbook and identify where subjects are covered in more detail in both your text and in your course syllabus. It should be seen as a framework in which to organise the subject matter, and to extract the most important points from your textbooks, lecture notes, and other learning materials on your course.

The Companion will also help you learn more efficiently, to anticipate exam questions, and understand what your examiners will be looking for. Learning is best accomplished by seeing the information from several different angles – which is why you attend lectures and tutorials, read the textbook, and read around the subject in general. This book will help you to bring together these different sources.

How to use this book

This book should be used as a supplement to your textbook and lecture notes. You may want to glance through it quickly, reading it in parallel with your course syllabus and textbook, and note where each topic is covered in both the syllabus and this Companion. Ideally, you will have already bought this book before your course starts, so that you can get a quick overview of each topic before you go into a lecture or read a textbook chapter – but if you didn't do this, all is not lost. The Companion will still be equally helpful as a revision guide.

The first section is about how to think like a management accountant: it will help you to get into the mindset of the subject and think about it critically. As a bonus this section will help you to understand why examination questions so often require a discussion or report to management, in which clear communication of ideas and options is important. Some running themes are also set out – these concern issues that arise often, and can often be brought into examination answers.

Part 2 goes into the curriculum in more detail, taking each topic and providing you with the key elements. Again, this does not substitute for the deeper coverage you will have had in your lectures and texts, but it does provide a quick revision guide, or a 'primer' to use before lectures.

You can use this book either to give yourself a head start before you start studying management accounting, in other words give yourself a preview course, or it can be used as a revision aid, or of course both. Each chapter in Part 2 contains the following features:

- **Tips** which are reminders of important points or help you to answer examination questions.
- **Numerical examples** which illustrate the main calculations you might be asked to perform in an examination. All examples are followed by worked answers, sometimes with commentary.
- **Taking it further** ideas. These often introduce some criticality, perhaps asking you to think about the complications of real-life practice or consider a topic from a broader perspective.
- **Textbook guides** will direct you to chapters from major textbooks that build on what has been covered in each of the Companion's chapters in Part 2.

Part 3 of this Companion is a study guide which will help you with getting the most from your studies in general, with revising for the management accounting exam, and with approaching the exam itself.

A glossary of key terms is included at the back of the book. Key terms have been **highlighted** throughout.

Thinking like a management accountant

Advice to someone starting a career in management accounting might go something like this:

You will often be the main numbers person in an organisation. Much of your work will be routine, though you may be able to improve presentation to make your output more intelligible.

You will have occasional requests for special reports or opportunities to research and report on a topic. You must obtain clear instructions and check with the person commissioning the work that you agree on the scope and purpose – if the person you are dealing with is not an accountant, you may in effect be speaking different languages.

It will be your responsibility to gather all the information you need – the sources you are directed to may be insufficient or incomplete and things people tell you may be out of date or wrong.

You will usually find that your numerical skills are adequate for the work you need to do, but when you are doing work of an unusual kind, or work you have not done before, your biggest challenge will be to think clearly and ensure, for example, that you consider only those costs that are relevant. It is worth spending whatever time is necessary to do this.

Clarity is vital in reporting: if the reader misunderstands your report, it is your fault. Use short words and avoid awkward constructions like double negatives ('It is reasonable to assume ...', may not convey exactly the same nuance as 'It is not unreasonable to assume ...', but it is easier to understand); use graphs to summarise numbers; explain the significance of numbers.

Oral presentations may be required. They are not opportunities to show how clever you are, nor to humiliate other managers. Even if someone asks what may appear to be a foolish question, you should answer in such a way as to make the question appear useful. Remember that you may have a tendency to focus on numbers and that, especially in an oral presentation, verbal explanations are vital.

Much of the time your reports will form a basis for others to make decisions; you will rarely be the decision maker early in your career.

This will not prevent people from attacking you. A typical complaint may be, 'I had this great idea which would have made the company a fortune, but the bean-counters couldn't understand it'. If you have done your work properly, it is more likely that the 'great idea' would have been catastrophic for the company and that is why it was rejected. Get used to it and react with restraint and humour if at all.

Sometimes you will independently come up with a good idea. The most effective way to have it adopted is to spread it quietly and persistently until someone in authority appropriates it and pushes it through.

How can these ideas illuminate our understanding of the study of management accounting? Some themes emerge:

- The management accountant is not normally the decision maker, but provides information on which line managers can base their decisions. It is important to recognise this, if only because 'bean-counters' tend to get blamed for decisions – often by the very people who made those decisions! If an examiner asks for a recommendation to management on a situation, avoid expressing your answer as a decision – ultimately it will be up to management to decide, once they have read your recommendation.
- Communication is of great importance. You might even say that if the message fails to get through to the people it is aimed at, it has failed completely. It is important to recognise that not everyone feels comfortable thinking through numbers. This means that the management accountant has to work hard at clarity of expression, perhaps using graphs and other visual aids to promote understanding. In an exam answer the exact question, and make a numerical answer complete – take care to show that you understand by including units and a little text where appropriate. A calculation on its own, however perfect, will not earn full marks if the ultimate response to the question ('Should the company proceed with this project?') is not there.
- The importance of data quality – no matter how sophisticated is the calculation, it can never be better than the data on which it is based. This point may be worth making if you are asked in an exam to comment on the results of your calculations. Some of the most significant calculations are based on forecast data and this forecast had to be made by someone. Its quality will depend on that person's ability, objectivity and experience.
- Clear thinking – it is too easy to follow on doing things the way they have always been done in the organisation. Can reports be improved? Should they be produced at all? Are only **relevant costs** considered? In an exam irrelevant data is occasionally introduced, to tempt you to use it inappropriately. Also, does your answer pass the common-sense test? Will a project really make **profits** many times the size of the initial investment, or have you made an error in your arithmetic? Does it make sense to produce an answer to several decimal places when the data units are in thousands?

These concepts form the basis for running themes which underlie the work of management accountants.

First, *numeracy:* this is so fundamental that we will not refer to it again. You will rarely have to deal with anything more than simple arithmetic, and you will be able to use a calculator or spreadsheet if you wish, but you will need to have or acquire a facility for manipulating numbers and understanding the results. Numbers are the core of a management accountant's work.

Second, *clarity:* much of the time you will be doing routine work, but your main value to the organisation rests on those occasions when it is necessary to produce something out of the ordinary. At such times you will need to recognise which factors are relevant to the problem and which techniques to use. It is worth spending a little time to make sure your thinking is straight.

Finally, *communication:* you will often be working with people who are not accountants, and you will have to make them understand you. If they do not, it is your fault, not theirs, and the consequences for the organisation could be serious.

part two
core areas of the curriculum

1
determining cost

Key ideas

Revenues and costs

Every receipt by a firm is part of its revenues, and every expenditure is part of its costs. We need to analyse both revenues and costs in some detail so that, for example, we know whether an item we are selling is costing us more to make than its selling price.

Recording and analysis of revenues is comparatively simple, as the firm determines the goods and services it sells and records the revenue generated as part of the process of charging its customers. The expenditure side is more complex, and we will treat it in more detail.

The first step is to record all expenditure. The level of detail varies with the enterprise, but the principle is to record the maximum amount of detail that is required at the time and that may be foreseen to be required in the future, as it is expensive and slow to go back and analyse spending in new ways. A typical manufacturing firm will record labour costs, for example, in some depth (wages in each department split by basic wages, overtime, shift premium, sickness pay, national insurance costs, etc.).

For each kind of enterprise there are standard ways of recording costs and reporting them, so it is not necessary for each new company to invent its own methods.

> *Examples for management accounting are often set in the context of a manufacturing concern, because tangible outputs are easier to deal with. But don't forget that the context could be an organisation in another industry – for example service or construction – or a not-for-profit organisation.*

Having recorded costs, it is usually desirable to report on them in several ways.

The broadest view is the overall profit made in a period. In principle it is easy to calculate this, as the result is arrived at by deducting the costs incurred in a period from the revenues earned. In practice it is more complicated than it sounds to ensure that the appropriate costs are matched, the most difficult problem being the valuation of **stocks** of goods at the beginning and end of the period.

Cost information is also used for decision making, and it is important in that context to use only the relevant information and ignore the irrelevant. For example, if a cost is going to be incurred anyway, regardless of the decision taken, it is irrelevant for the decision. Wages and salaries are often costs of this type, if the individuals will still be employed regardless. Similarly, a cost which has already been incurred cannot be affected by the decision. Sometimes a cost – or receipt – will happen if only one course of action or other is taken, such as a receipt for the sale of equipment if a project is abandoned. Also, there may be an **opportunity cost** – making the decision one way will mean that some other course of action is ruled out, and revenue from that other action is lost.

> *It is important to consider each cost individually – remembering that in questions on this topic, 'red herring' items are often included to tempt you.*

It can be easier to draw up two lists of costs and receipts, one for each course of action under consideration. This takes extra time, however, so often only the difference between the two lists is shown as a solution. You should use whichever method you prefer – and for study purposes, why not use both and check that they lead to the same outcome?

EXAMPLE   Relevant and irrelevant costs

A company's IT department normally levies a charge of £12 per hour for work done by its technicians for external customers – other companies in the group, or staff and their friends.

A number of personal computers are to be replaced very shortly. These originally cost £36,000 and **depreciation** and maintenance charges have averaged £15,000 per annum over the three years of their life. Depreciation is charged at 25% per annum on a straight line basis. The computers could be sold off to staff for home use, which would earn revenue of £2,000 but would involve the IT department in 40 hours of work preparing them for sale and incur hardware costs of £900 for modems, missing leads and so on. Alternatively, the computers could be sent to a charity for disposal in which case the preparation work required of the IT department would amount to only 10 hours, but transport costs of £200 would be incurred. The manager of the IT department estimates that there are perhaps 20 hours of technician time available in the near future, before external work has to be turned down.

If the decision is made to give the computers to the charity, what is the cost? The situation can be summarised as follows:

	Staff	Charity
Income	2,000	0
Opportunity cost:		
Technician time @ £12 per hour	–240	0
Hardware costs	–900	
Transport costs	0	–200
Benefit	860	–200

In terms of the cost of the charitable donation, the cost could be shown like this:

Income forgone	2,000
Technician time saved	–240
Hardware costs saved	–900
Transport costs	200
Total	£1,060

This cost is, of course, the difference between the two options in the earlier table: £860 – (–£200) = £1,060.

Note that since 20 hours of technician time are available before external income has to be turned down, all the work can be done if the charity option is chosen. However if the computers are prepared for staff purchase, external work of 20 hours is an opportunity cost at £12 per hour. Also, the costs already incurred in buying and owning the computers are irrelevant – the only question now is how to dispose of them.

The running theme here is clarity – the numbers are not difficult to work with, but you need to choose the right ones.

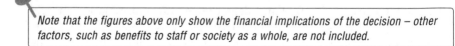

Note that the figures above only show the financial implications of the decision – other factors, such as benefits to staff or society as a whole, are not included.

Sunk costs

Sunk costs refer to any past expenditure that cannot be recovered, or a future expenditure that cannot be avoided. The significance of the term is that such costs should be ignored for decision making purposes.

While this may seem obvious in the abstract, people often fail to think clearly about sunk costs and make unwise decisions as a result.

> *A simple example may be familiar: you have bought a return rail ticket, but while at your destination a friend offers you a free lift home. This will be more convenient and quicker than taking the train but means you will have to throw away the return half of your ticket. What do you do?*

Naturally you accept the lift, but how can you rationalise the waste of half your fare? The point is that the whole cost of the ticket was a sunk cost as soon as you bought it. When you have to make a decision, there is no further cost to incur whatever you do, so you simply need to choose the best way to get home.

The error that you avoided here is one that seems easy to fall into on a larger scale. A typical comment might be, 'We have spent so much on project A that we have no choice but to continue'.

Another error is best illustrated by an example.

EXAMPLE   A local council is renovating a building, and has spent £100,000 so far. A new contractor offers an alternative, cheaper method

The relevant figures are:

	£
Current method	
Spent so far	100,000
Needed to finish	60,000
New method	
Total cost	80,000

So the new method offers a saving of £80,000, but should the council switch to it? Obviously the answer is no, as switching would cost an extra £20,000.

> *It is usually quite easy to deal correctly with sunk costs: once you have spotted the problem the answer is not hard to find. However the problem is a behavioural one, and the contribution of the accountant is to provide a statement revealing the cost of alternative outcomes, so that the decision can be made on a rational basis. There is no guarantee that this is what will happen!*

Marginal cost of a product

It may also be useful to know the **marginal cost** of a product. This is the total cost of making one more unit. As long as the number of units remains within the **relevant range** – the range within which assumptions about cost behaviour are valid – then marginal cost is the same as **variable cost**. Outside this range the marginal cost may vary.

Take the sale of coach tickets as an example. The variable cost of one extra passenger may be calculated in terms of fuel and so on. The **fixed cost** is irrelevant to the marginal cost as long as seats are available on the coach. However if a further ticket is sold – and if the company is obliged to honour it – an extra coach must be run, with its attendant fixed costs. The marginal (extra) cost of that further ticket is much higher as a result. In this case, marginal cost is not the same as variable cost.

EXAMPLE Fixed and variable costs

A government normally requires motorists to purchase an annual licence for each car on the road, at a cost of £180. There is a proposal to take advantage of new technology to change to a basis of charging road tax at £0.03 per mile travelled. For a particular make of car, costs per annum are estimated at £3,000 and insurance costs at £300. Maintenance charges at are estimated at £100 for every 5,000 miles. Petrol costs £0.80 per litre and consumption averages 6 miles per litre. What are the annual costs of the car for mileages of 4,000, 14,000 and 24,000 miles per annum?

Licence on annual basis: *Annual mileage*

	4,000	14,000	24,000
	£	£	£
Maintenance	80	280	480
Petrol	533	1,867	3,200
Total variable cost	613	2,147	3,680
Vehicle licence (annual basis)	180	180	180
Depreciation	3,500	3,500	3,500
Insurance	300	300	300
Total fixed cost	3,980	3,980	3,980
Total cost	4,593	6,127	7,660
Variable cost per mile	0.153	0.153	0.153
Fixed cost per mile	0.995	0.284	0.166
Total cost per mile	1.148	0.438	0.319

Road tax on mileage basis: *Annual mileage*

	4,000	14,000	24,000
	£	£	£
Road tax (mileage basis)	140	490	840
Maintenance	80	280	480
Petrol	533	1,867	3,200
Total variable cost	753	2,637	4,520
Depreciation	3,500	3,500	3,500
Insurance	300	300	300
Total fixed cost	3,800	3,800	3,800
Total cost	4,553	6,437	8,320
Variable cost per mile	0.188	0.188	0.188
Fixed cost per mile	0.950	0.271	0.158
Total cost per mile	1.138	0.460	0.347

As the annual mileage rises, the mileage basis for the tax gets more expensive for the motorist than the annual basis.

Cost and volume

Cost-volume-profit analysis

It is useful, often vital, for us to know how our costs vary with volume of production. It is obvious that as output increases costs will go up, but the exact relationship is important.

We use **CVP** to analyse cost behaviour within a small range (the relevant range) where we expect to operate in the short term. Within this range it is acceptable and useful to assume that some costs are fixed (for example, rent, rates) and that other costs (for example, materials) vary directly with output. We can also reasonably assume that revenue is directly related to output.

With these assumptions, there are some results that can be represented on a simple straight-line graph.

EXAMPLE   Cost-volume-profit analysis

An inspirational speaker is planning to hold a seminar in a city hotel. The room hire for the day will be £500, advertising and the speaker's travelling expenses will be £300, and the hotel will charge £20 per head for coffee and lunch. A similar seminar in another city attracted 50 participants.

At a fee of £100 per participant, we can draw a chart as follows:

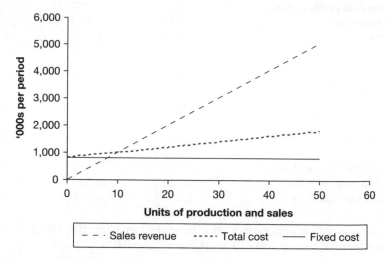

Figure 2.1   Break-even chart

The **break-even point**, where the lines representing sales revenue and total cost intersect, can be read from the chart as occurring at a level of 10 units, which means 10 participants must pay if a **loss**-making situation is to be avoided.

Usually a numerical analysis is more accurate. For the seminar example, we can ask several questions and calculate answers as follows:

Q1 If the planned seminar attracts 50 participants, what profit will be made if a fee of £100 per participant is charged?

Note: for all questions except Q5, fixed costs total £800 for the day.

A straightforward calculation of profit:

Revenue (50 × 100)	*5,000*
Room hire and other fixed costs	*800*
Coffee and lunches (50 × 20)	*1,000*
Profit	*3,200*

Q2 How many participants must be attracted to break-even at a fee of £100 per participant?

The variable cost for each participant is £20, and therefore the **contribution** from each participant to fixed cost is £(100−20) = £80

Fixed cost is £800 so the number of participants needed to break even is £(800/20) = 10 people.
 Check this:

Revenue (10 × 100)	*1,000*
Less variable costs:	
Coffee and lunches (10 × 20)	*200*
Contribution	*800*
Less fixed costs:	
Room hire and other fixed costs	*800*
Difference = profit	*0*

Q3 If a profit of £2,000 for the day is required, what fee must be charged to each of 50 participants?

Required profit	*2,000*
Room hire and other fixed costs	*800*
Contribution required	*2,800*
Add variable costs:	
Coffee and lunches (50 × 20)	*1,000*
Total = revenue	*3,800*
The fee per participant is (3,800/50) = £76	

Q4 If a profit of £2,000 for the day is required but the maximum feasible fee is thought to be £100, how many participants must be attracted?

Required profit	*2,000*
Room hire and other fixed costs	*800*
Total = contribution	*2,800*

The contribution per participant is £80 (see Q2)
 The required number of participants is (2,800/80) = 35 people

Q5 If the speaker takes his personal assistant at a cost of £150 for the day but wishes to maintain the same level of profit, how many extra participants must be attracted at a fee of £100 per participant?
 The extra fixed costs to be covered are £150 and the contribution per participant is £80. £(150/80) = 1.875 so two additional participants are required.

Sometimes an answer won't work out exactly! Where 'units' – such as people – are indivisible you still need to return a sensible answer, so round up to the next whole number. The resulting profit might be slightly higher than the target but at least your answer makes sense.

Q6 On the basis of the facts in Q1, how far can the number of participants fall from the expected level before a loss is made? What is this fall as a percentage of the expected number?

The expected level of sales is 50 participants and the break even level is 10 people (Q2). So the **margin of safety** is 40 people, or (40/50) = 80%.

For many reasons, such analysis is only useful over a small range of output for a limited time. For example, if output doubles demand may not keep up and it may be necessary to reduce prices. On the input side, it may be necessary to pay overtime rates or supplies of material may be limited.

The running theme of communication suggests that the graphical answer, while not displaying the same degree of accuracy as the numbers themselves, may make your explanation easier to follow.

Direct and indirect costs

One of the most useful classifications of costs, especially in manufacturing, is that of **direct** and **indirect costs.**

Direct costs are those which can be allocated to a particular item. It is comparatively easy to calculate the cost of materials used to make an item, or the time spent by an operator on a machine to produce it.

Indirect costs are those which cannot be so allocated, for example the cost of a factory manager's salary or the rent of the factory where the item is made.

In manufacturing, all products are costed in detail using a cost card, so called because it used to be a piece of card. Obviously it is now more efficient to keep the information on computer, but the concept has not changed.

Here is an example of a cost card:

	£
Direct materials:	
1.5 kg of A at £5 per kg	*7.50*
2.5 kg of B at £4 per kg	*10.00*
Direct labour (1.2 hours at £8 per hour)	*9.60*
Variable overhead (1.2 hours at £1 per direct labour hour)	*1.20*
Total standard variable cost	*28.30*

In addition to direct costs it is necessary to arrive at a way of allocating indirect costs to arrive at the total cost of a product. Traditionally this was done quite approximately, spreading indirect costs according to the amount of **direct labour** or machine hours used, for example. Currently firms try to allocate indirect costs more accurately to the activities that cause them using **activity-based costing**.

Taking it **FURTHER**

The ideas in this chapter are basic to management accounting, yet they are not at all easy to apply in practice. Even if good quality data can be obtained – what is the cost per litre of petrol, actually? – uncertainties remain. Is our selling price straightforward, or does it vary according to market or volume? What is the relevant range for a given cost? Will prices be similar next year, or next week? As a thought experiment, estimate the costs of flying a passenger from London to Glasgow.

Textbook Guide

2	
costing systems	

Types of costing system

We need a method of applying costs to products for several reasons. The least demanding is the reporting of financial results for the whole enterprise. We could do this even without detailed knowledge of costs except for the question of stock. The reason is that some of our expenditure in a period is not related to sales of that period, so we need a consistent method of valuing stocks at the start and end of the period. This applies not only to manufacturing but to other processes, such as construction or software engineering.

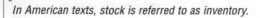

> In American texts, stock is referred to as inventory.

A more important reason for applying costs to products is for decision making. It is vital, for example, to know whether a product is profitable or not.

Variable costing provides an acceptable method of valuing stock for the purpose of reporting profit. **Variable costs** are those that vary with the level of production, for example, material, direct labour and variable overhead.

Variable costing may also be useful in short term decisions. In the short term, a company will gain by selling its products for more than their variable cost of production rather than not selling them at all.

However, in the longer term this would lead to disaster if the contribution to fixed costs were insufficient. If a company is faced with market prices below the full cost of production, selling at prices which more than cover variable costs but fall short of full cost is only a short term expedient.

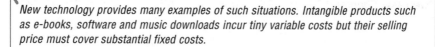

> New technology provides many examples of such situations. Intangible products such as e-books, software and music downloads incur tiny variable costs but their selling price must cover substantial fixed costs.

EXAMPLE

Number of widgets per month		5,000	
		Direct cost basis	Absorption costing
Materials	5,000	5,000	5,000
Direct labour	3,000	3,000	3,000
Per month			
Indirect labour	1,200		1,200
Factory overhead	1,000		1,000
Total per 5,000 widgets		8,000	10,200
Per widget		1.60	2.04

- *Which cost should we take for pricing purposes?*
Normally we would take the higher cost as a guide in order to cover all our costs. However, suppose we have no other product line at the moment and the highest price we can get is (say) £1.95. It will be worth continuing to make the product in the short term even at this lower price since the line is making some contribution, at least, to fixed costs.
- *How should we value any stock remaining unsold at the end of the month?*
Normally we would use absorption cost.
- *How does the choice of system affect reported profit?*
In the very long term reported profit is not affected, but the choice of system does affect the profit in successive accounting periods. For example, if closing stocks are high, under the **absorption costing** method they will have a high value and so reported profit is increased in this period but reduced in the next.
- *What happens if more than 5,000 widgets are produced in any month?*
Using direct costs there is no difference. Using absorption costing, the cost per unit will be lower because the costs of **indirect labour** and factory overhead will be spread over more units.

The standard costing system

The **standard costing** system is covered in detail in Chapter 6.

Standard costing systems are widely used in manufacturing but rarely used elsewhere. The main ideas are:

- A standard cost represents expectations of the cost for a single unit of product, and includes costs such as materials, labour and machine time.
- The standard cost is developed through experience and observation of manufacture of that item, or might be derived from experience and observation of the manufacture of a similar item if the product is a new one.
- The original impetus for the development of standard costing was a drive for efficiency but standard costs are also a useful tool for other purposes such as valuing **inventory**, controlling costs and setting **budgets**.
- Direct costs such as materials and labour are always included in standard cost but production-related **overheads** may also be included in an absorption costing system. These will be overheads such as machine power, factory rent and rates and production salaries. We would exclude costs which are not related to production such as administration salaries.
- These variable overhead costs are allocated according to some more direct measure of activity level, such as labour hours or machine hours, whichever seems the most appropriate.
- Once standard costs have been determined for all products, then direct costs and variable overheads can be calculated for the planned production in the budget period.

- Standard costs are also used for control purposes and have significant motivational effects. Ideally standards are challenging but if they are not in fact attainable, budgets will not be attained either.

Note that:

- An absorption costing system requires that indirect manufacturing costs (as well as direct manufacturing costs, of course) are included in the cost of products for purposes of calculating the cost of manufacture.
- The unit cost for each product is required for calculating stocks and work in progress. The unit cost under an absorption costing system will be different from the unit cost under a variable costing system.
- Therefore, the choice of system affects the period profit.
- In the long run (perhaps several years) the choice of system makes no difference since variations in one period are counterbalanced by variations in another period.
- A marginal costing system is also known as a **variable** or **direct** costing system

EXAMPLE

A new product is launched in January and sells for £18. Sales of 300,000 units per month are expected. The variable cost per unit is £14, manufacturing overheads are budgeted at £510,000 per month and non-manufacturing overheads are budgeted at £200,000 per month. For the first six months sales are fairly even, though an advertising promotion in late March does produce a modest boost in sales.

Units (000s)	Jan	Feb	Mar	Apr	May	June	Total
Sold	300	300	300	320	330	310	1,860
Produced	300	300	330	360	290	300	1,880

To prepare profit statements, the closing stock at the end of the whole six month period is first calculated. From the table above it is evident that there is some closing stock:

> Produced (1,880) – Sold (1,860) = 20 left in stock at the end of July.

(Actually this is 20,000 units but we will continue to work in thousands.) However we need to know closing stock for each period, not just the end of the six months.

We can assume that the opening stock is nil since we have no information on its level – and this seems feasible since the product was only launched in January.

Units (000s)	Jan	Feb	Mar	Apr	May	June
Opening stock	0	0	0	30	70	30
Units produced	300	300	330	360	290	300
Units sold	300	300	300	320	330	310
Closing stock	0	0	30	70	30	20

To calculate the value of the closing stock for each month, we just calculate the stock level at the variable cost given in the question – for example in March:

$30 \times 14 = 420$

Variable costing statement

000s	Jan	Feb	Mar	Apr	May	June
Opening stock	0	0	0	420	980	420
Production cost	4,200	4,200	4,620	5,040	4,060	4,200
Closing stock	0	0	420	980	420	280
Cost of sales	4,200	4,200	4,200	4,480	4,620	4,340
Fixed costs	510	510	510	510	510	510
Total costs	4,710	4,710	4,710	4,990	5,130	4,850
Sales	5,400	5,400	5,400	5,760	5,940	5,580
Gross profit	690	690	690	770	810	730
Less non-manufacturing costs	200	200	200	200	200	200
Net profit	490	490	490	570	610	530

Total profit or loss						3,180

Fixed manufacturing costs have been added each month to the cost of sales, to give total costs. Fixed *non*-manufacturing costs, in contrast, have been deducted monthly from gross profit.

For the absorption costing statement, we wish to absorb fixed manufacturing cost into the unit product cost.

We can calculate the fixed manufacturing cost per unit by spreading the total monthly cost of £510,000 over the monthly activity level of 300,000 units:

$510,000/300,000 = £1.70$ per unit.

To value stocks and cost of sales we can now add the variable cost of £14 to give a cost of £15.70 per unit. The fixed cost of £1.70 per unit is also used to adjust the cost of sales for under- or over-absorption in months when sales differ from the planned level of 300,000 units.

Absorption costing statement

000s	Jan	Feb	Mar	Apr	May	June
Opening stock	0	0	0	471	1099	471
Production cost	4,710	4,710	5,181	5,652	4,553	4,710
Closing stock	0	0	471	1,099	471	314
Cost of sales	4,710	4,710	4,710	5,024	5,181	4,867
COS adjustments	0	0	−51	−102	17	0
Total costs	4,710	4,710	4,659	4,922	5,198	4,867
Sales	5,400	5,400	5,400	5,760	5,940	5,580
Gross profit	690	690	741	838	742	713
Less non-manufacturing costs	200	200	200	200	200	200
Net profit	490	490	541	638	542	513
Total profit or loss						3,214

If we compare the profit for the whole six month period, we can see that the absorption costing statement shows a larger profit:

$3,214 - 3,180 = a\ difference\ of\ 34$

This difference is in fact the amount of fixed manufacturing cost included in the valuation of the 20,000 units of closing stock in the absorption costing statement:

$20,000\ @\ £1.70 = £34,000$

> Note that fixed non-manufacturing costs are never absorbed – they are treated in the same way whether the system is based on variable or absorption cost accounting. Check the two costing statements to see that the fixed non-manufacturing cost has been deducted from gross profit in both cases.

Activity-based costing (ABC)

Some overheads are related to volume of output, where others are not. If costs are allocated purely on the basis of one of two chosen cost factors (for example machine hour or labour hour), they may not reflect the activities actually involved and each activity's use of resources. For example, in a printing firm if overheads are allocated simply on the basis of machine hour (for example) then the short-run job will appear to cost very little compared to a long-run job. However the short-run job will still need to incur lead-in costs such as a quotation, artwork, separation, plate-making, proofing and so on, and these 'per job' costs will be under-represented. At the same time, the costs will be over-represented on the long-run job. Activities that incur significant costs are called cost *drivers*, and it is necessary to calculate a rate for each one.

> *Think about the effect of accounting systems and techniques on the decisions that people take – this idea is at the very heart of management accounting. In the printing firm, what could be the consequences of inaccurate information about the use of resources on different print jobs?*

EXAMPLE

A printing firm estimates figures for the current year as follows:

Non-machine job-related costs	
(quotation, artwork etc. as above)	*36,000 per month*
Average number of jobs per month	*200*

There are 6 machines, each operating for 240 hours per month so there are 1,440 machine hours available per month.
This is 36,000/1,440 = £25 per machine hour.
   Alternatively, this could be expressed as (36,000/200) = £180 per job.
   A small job takes 1 machine hour, and another job in the same week takes 40 hours machine time.
   On the traditional basis the charge for non-machine costs would be:

Small job 1 × 25 = £25
Large job 40 × 25 = 1,000

On an **ABC** basis both jobs would attract the same charge = £180.
   This is a significant difference. It makes small jobs look less expensive than they really are – and could encourage staff to book in loss-making jobs. At the same time large profitable jobs will look more expensive than they really are – and the firm could lose business to other firms with a better grasp of the cost realities.

The ABC system compared with a traditional system

A company produces three main products. As an exercise the current system for allocation of overheads, based on direct labour hours, is to be compared with an ABC system.

Figures for the three products for a given month are as follows:

	Product X	Product Y	Product Z
Production and sales (units)	10,000	20,000	30,000
Direct material cost	10	14	6
Direct labour hours	1.5	2.5	0.5
Direct labour cost	10.5	17.5	3.5
Machine hours	1.75	2	0.75
Number of production runs	32	8	16
Number of receipts	45	4	15
Number of production orders	40	7	25

Overhead costs are as follows:

Set-up	70,000
Machines	300,000
Receiving	45,000
Laboratory cost	60,000

Most of the cost driver rates for an ABC system have been computed (all costs in £s):

Machine overhead rate – per machine hour	3.75
Cost per machine set-up	1,250
Cost per order for raw materials ordered and received	703

An additional cost driver rate, for engineering and laboratory services, is to be computed on the basis of a total monthly cost of £60,000 and allocated according to the number of production orders for each product.

To apply a cost, first calculate the cost driver rate (that is, the cost per unit of activity in the relevant period). For engineering and laboratory services, we have a total cost per month, and the unit of activity is the production order. We can find out how many production orders there were in the month from the first table in this example. Once we have the rate, the overhead per unit of product can be calculated. Find the total cost for that product over the period, and divide by the number of units.

Workings

We calculate cost per unit first on a traditional basis, then on the basis of the ABC drivers described above.

Direct labour hour basis:

	Product X	Product Y	Product Z	Total
Labour hours in period	15,000	50,000	15,000	80,000
Direct labour	10.50	17.50	3.50	
Direct materials	10.00	14.00	6.00	Rate
Set-up	1.31	2.19	0.44	0.88
Machines	5.63	9.38	1.88	3.75
Receiving	0.84	1.41	0.28	0.56
Laboratory cost	1.13	1.88	0.38	0.75
Total cost per unit	29.41	46.34	12.47	

For each overhead, a rate is calculated based on total labour hours. For example, the set-up cost is calculated as £70,000/80,000 hours = £0.88 per labour hour. It is then applied to each product according to the labour hours used to make the product:

Product X: £0.88 × 1.5 = £1.31 per unit

ABC basis:

Calculating the final cost driver rate:

£60,000/72 = £833 per production order.

	Product X	Product Y	Product Z
Direct labour	10.50	17.50	3.50
Direct materials	10.00	14.00	6.00
Set-up	4.00	0.50	0.67
Machines	6.56	7.50	2.81
Receiving	3.16	0.14	0.35
Laboratory cost	3.33	0.29	0.69
Total cost per unit	37.56	39.93	14.03

Direct labour and materials costs are the same as for the traditional calculation. However for each overhead, a different amount is now calculated based on the cost drivers. Here are some examples.

Machine set-up for product X:
The cost per set-up is £1,250 and there were 32 production runs for the 10000 units made of this product.
£1,250 × 32/10,000 = £4 per unit

Machine overheads for product X:
The overhead rate is £4 per machine hour and product X takes 1.75 machine hours to make:
£3.75 × 1.75 = £6.56 per unit

Receiving cost for product Y:
The receiving cost per order is £703 and there were 4 receipts for the 20,000
units made of this product.
£703 × 4/20,000 = £0.14 per unit.

Laboratory cost for product Z:
The laboratory cost per order is £833 and there were 25 production orders for
the 30,000 units of this product.
£833 × 25/30,000 = £0.69 per unit

Now we can see how the traditional basis and the ABC basis compare:

	Product X	*Product Y*	*Product Z*
Direct labour hours basis	*29.41*	*46.34*	*12.47*
ABC basis	*37.56*	*39.93*	*14.03*

The costs for product Y no longer seem so high compared to the other two products.
If we look again at how product Y uses resources:

	Product X	*Product Y*	*Product Z*
Production and sales (units)	*10,000*	*20,000*	*30,000*
Direct material cost	*10*	*14*	*6*
Direct labour hours	*1.5*	*2.5*	*0.5*
Direct labour cost	*10.5*	*17.5*	*3.5*
Machine hours	*1.75*	*2*	*0.75*
Number of production runs	*32*	*8*	*16*
Number of receipts	*45*	*4*	*15*
Number of production orders	*40*	*7*	*25*

Product Y direct costs may be high but it seems that it is produced by infrequent, long production runs with infrequent deliveries of raw materials. Compared to the other two products, product Y is a light consumer of overheads.

 Taking it **FURTHER**

An electronics firm makes a wide range of products, and many of the products incorporate standard parts. The firm implements an ABC system in which the overhead rate associated with purchasing parts varies according to the total volume used, so that standard parts incur much less overhead than novel ones. If you were a product designer for the firm, how would this system affect your choice of parts? What might be the long-term effect on product design?

Textbook Guide

3	
product mix	

We often have to decide which products to make – or which services to offer. For example, a toy manufacturer needs to have products which are popular and available in the shops at the right time – before Christmas, perhaps. Some toys will fade in popularity and others may achieve unexpected success if they become a craze. The manufacturer needs to make decisions constantly about which toys to develop, make or discontinue – and how many to make of each product line.

What is the basis for such decisions? Important considerations will be forecast demand – at varying prices – and forecast profit, which means that the company needs to have for each product line:

* accurate estimates of costs – which means that costs must be accurately recorded;
* accurate calculations of profit;
* an effective system for calculating cost for new products at varying production levels; and
* in some cases, forecasts of future currency exchange rates.

We also need to know how much to make of each product where there is plenty of demand but some element of the resources is limited – for example, there are only so many machines available.

Sometimes we may be able to improve profit by **sub-contracting** some element of the process – for example, buying a component in rather than making it ourselves.

We may be able to distinguish between different types of customer. To maximise profit we may choose to focus our efforts on one group of customers at the expense of others – or even to ignore one group of customers altogether.

Discontinuing a product

It is important to be careful when choosing whether or not to continue making a given product line on the grounds of profitability. The method of determining profit for that line could make the difference between an apparently profitable line, and one which should be discontinued.

Other points to consider are:

- Are the conditions which make the product unprofitable temporary or permanent? For example, materials cost.
- Market conditions – what sales are anticipated?

EXAMPLE Discontinuance

A company makes two similar products, A and B. A profit statement has been produced for the last quarter which seems to show that the more expensive product should be discontinued.

	A	B	Total
Production and sales – units (000s)	30	10	
Sales price (£s)	45	55	
	£000s	£000s	£000s
Sales revenue	1,350	550	1,900
Cost of sales	900	480	1,380
Gross profit	450	70	520
Sales and distribution costs	140	70	210
Administration costs	160	50	210
Net profit or loss	150	–50	100

Further enquiries reveal that only 70% of the figures shown for cost of sales is variable cost, and of the remainder, only half is product specific. Other costs are all confirmed to be fixed costs, but 20% of sales and distribution costs, and 10% of administration costs, are product specific.

> The idea here is to recast the profit statement to clearly show contribution (instead of gross profit). To do this, ensure that the cost of sales figure includes only variable cost and deduct from sales. The fixed costs are now divided up into two parts. The product specific costs can be deducted from sales for each product. However general fixed costs – which will still be incurred if product B is dropped – are not separated by product but grouped and deducted from total contribution to give the net profit or loss for the whole enterprise.

For example:

- The calculation for cost of sales for product A is 70% of 900,000 = £630,000.
- Sales and distribution for product B is 20% of 70,000 = £14,000.
- General administration costs are 90% of 210,000 = £189,000.

	A	B	Total
	£000s	*£000s*	*£000s*
Sales revenue	1,350	550	1,900
Cost of sales (variable)	630	336	966
Sales margin	720	214	934
Product-specific costs			
Cost of sales (other)	135	72	207
Sales and distribution	28	14	42
Administration	16	5	21
Contribution	541	123	664
General costs			
Cost of sales			207
Sales and distribution			168
Administration			189
Net profit or loss			100

Now it is evident that product B makes a positive contribution of £123,000 to fixed costs and should be retained. To demonstrate this, you can calculate what will happen if product B is in fact dropped:

Product A only	£000s
Sales revenue	1,350
Cost of sales (variable)	630
Sales margin	720
Product-specific costs	
Cost of sales (other)	135
Sales and distribution	28
Administration	16
Contribution	541
General costs	
Cost of sales	207
Sales and distribution	168
Administration	189
Net profit or loss	−23

With product A's contribution only, and the same general fixed costs, a loss is made.

The running themes here are clarity and communication – you will need to think carefully about which costs are relevant and then explain your conclusions with reasons why the usual calculations of profit are inappropriate.

Make or buy

Normally the element to be sub-contracted or bought in, is not core to the process – in order that problems do not have serious consequences. The element needs to be easily managed and not complex. For example distribution or warehousing could be outsourced, or a spare part purchased rather than made.

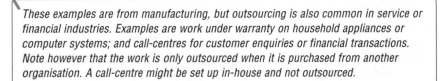

> These examples are from manufacturing, but outsourcing is also common in service or financial industries. Examples are work under warranty on household appliances or computer systems; and call-centres for customer enquiries or financial transactions. Note however that the work is only outsourced when it is purchased from another organisation. A call-centre might be set up in-house and not outsourced.

The decision to buy in rather than continue to supply 'in-house' assumes that you have some more profitable use for your resources. The approach to the problem is to determine cost to make the part or perform the service in-house, and compare this with the cost of buying in or outsourcing. Accurate costs are obviously important, and these should include time spent in managing the process for the outsourcing option.

EXAMPLE   Make or buy

A manufacturer can outsource manufacture of a component at a price of £45 per unit. Currently costs are estimated as follows:

	Cost £000s	Per unit £
Direct costs		
Materials	100	20
Labour	60	12
Manufacturing overheads		
Variable	15	3
Fixed	40	8
General overheads	30	6
Total cost	245	49

It looks as if the outsourced price of £45 will make the arrangement beneficial. However, it is found that of the fixed manufacturing overhead only 40% is product-specific. General overheads are not relevant for the decision in any case. When the costs are restated and compared with the costing of buying in, it is evident that the arrangement will not be beneficial:

	Make	Buy
Purchase cost		225
Direct costs		
Materials	100	
Labour	60	
Product-specific manufacturing overheads		
Variable	15	
Fixed	16	
Total cost	191	225

This analysis assumes however that there is no profitable use for the capacity released by outsourcing. If there is, then the contribution forgone should be added to the cost of the manufacturing option before it is compared with the outsourcing option.

> Consider the consequences over time of the decision to outsource. For example, special skills may be lost, or the conditions for purchase (such as the price for buying in) could change.

Optimum mix under conditions of limited capacity

Firms will normally try to produce goods or offer services according to perceived demand. However sometimes it may not be possible to produce according to demand because some resource is in scarce supply – for example, a raw material or component, or programming expertise. Given this limitation on capacity, the firm must decide how much of each product to produce to make the best profit it can. The general approach here is to determine for each product, the contribution per unit of the scarce resource – for example, £s per programmer-hour. Now the products can be ranked in order from the one which shows the highest contribution per programmer-hour, to the one which shows the lowest. Production is allocated to each product in rank order until the programmer-hours run out.

EXAMPLE Optimum mix

In this example the **limiting factor** is labour hours. Only 15,000 hours are available in December and the problem is to decide how much of the four products should be made to maximise profit. Variable manufacturing overheads such as machine expenses are recovered according to the labour hours worked, at the rate of £1 for every hour. The cost of materials, and the labour hours required, vary for each product.

	A	B	C	D
Maximum production (units)	2,500	4,000	1,200	4,000
Selling price per unit (£)	34	22	45	27
Material (£)	8	7	9	12
Skilled labour (hours)	2	1	3	1.5

The hourly rate for labour is £8 and fixed costs for December are budgeted at £20,000.

	A £	B £	C £	D £
Selling price	34	22	45	27
Materials	8	7	9	12
Labour	16	8	24	12
Variable overhead	2	1	3	1.5
Total variable cost	26	16	36	25.5
Contribution per unit	8	6	9	1.5
Contribution per labour hour	4	6	3	1
Ranking	2	1	3	4

Once contribution per unit has been determined, contribution per labour hour is calculated and the products ranked. Product B is the most profitable and product D the least profitable. The 15,000 available hours are now allocated to the products in rank order, until they run out.

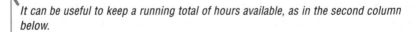

It can be useful to keep a running total of hours available, as in the second column below.

Allocation	Skilled hours available	Hours	Units	Contribution (£)
Product B	15,000	4,000	4,000	24,000
Product A	11,000	5,000	2,500	20,000

Product C	6,000	3,600	1,200	10,800
Product D	2,400	2,400	1,600	2,400
Total				57,200
Fixed costs				20,000
Profit				37,200

4,000 units of product D could be sold, but only 2,400 are made since this solution maximises contribution. Other products are made to maximum production levels.

If there is more than one constraint more complex methods must be used to solve the problem.

Linear programming is a mathematical technique that can deal with any number of constraints. A 'model' is constructed from the constraints and solved so as to optimise an objective – for example to minimise costs or in this case, to maximise contribution. In order to see which constraints define the region bounding feasible solutions, a graph is often drawn. However the number of alternatives (products, for example) is limited to two if the graphical method is used, as the graph will have only two axes. Once the relevant constraints are identified the optimum solution can be found by solving a series of simultaneous equations.

The **simplex algorithm** is a suitable method where there are more than two alternatives (products). This requires a computer which peforms many calculations to converge on the optimum solution. You can also use the Excel® add-in 'Solver' which is an integral part of the standard Excel installation. You need to specify the 'objective function', or goal, which in this case will be to maximise total contribution.

Decision trees

A **decision tree** can be used to set out alternative courses of action clearly so that a decision can be made. Each 'twig' has associated with it an outcome normally expressed in financial terms, the probability of that outcome occurring, and a financial value which is the product of the outcome and the probability. These products are summed to give the *expected outcome* for that branch of the tree. It is possible that the 'expected value' of a decision will not be identical to the actual outcome once that decision is made. In fact it is possible that the expected value is different from all the projected outcomes.

Where an outcome is not known with certainty, a probability is estimated.

If you are asked to comment on this process, remember that someone had to estimate the probabilities. In the example below, the marketing manager and the purchasing manager might have been asked to do so, for example. The calculations based on those estimates can only be as good as the estimates they made.

You compare the expected values for the branches which represent decision options. In this simple example, the decision is whether or not to proceed with a new product line, which is expected to have a short life but could prove popular. Probabilities have been assigned to sales volumes and to variable cost, which is uncertain as volume discounts have not yet been negotiated. A probability of 0.1 represents a 10% chance of occurrence, for example.

Sales volume	Units	Probability
Best	9,000	0.1
Most likely	7,000	0.8
Worst	6,000	0.1

Variable cost	£	Probability
Best	3.00	0.2
Most likely	4.00	0.6
Worst	5.00	0.2

From a selling price of £10 per unit and the figures for variable cost, contribution can be calculated. Note that the probabilities of the nine outcomes should add up to 1, and that the positive total expected value can be used as evidence that the product is worth producing.

Demand	Probability	Contribution	Probability	Joint probability	Expected value
9,000	0.1	7.00	0.2	0.02	1,260
		6.00	0.6	0.06	3,240
		5.00	0.2	0.02	900
7,000	0.8	7.00	0.2	0.16	7,840
		6.00	0.6	0.48	20,160
		5.00	0.2	0.16	5,600
6,000	0.1	7.00	0.2	0.02	840
		6.00	0.6	0.06	2,160
		5.00	0.2	0.02	600
Total				1.00	42,600

In tune with the running themes of both clarity and communication, it may be worth setting out your conclusions in graphical form.

Pricing

Possible methods include **cost plus**, prices determined by the market, and target cost, the last two being variations on the same theme. Market cost is seeing what the market will pay, while target cost is seeing what the market will pay, but then working back to cost via a known multiplier.

For the cost plus basis, determine cost and add a percentage margin. This is usually used for a one-off project where there is no obvious market price – normally on a basis agreed with the customer, since allowable elements of the cost will be determined by a contract. It will only be used where there is no market price available. This was formerly the standard way of pricing unique products, for example military equipment.

Market price is the most used but sometimes there is no market price available – for example, a new product – so one might use cost plus or guess what the maximum price could be. An important aim in establishing a market price is to try to position the product in a market which will produce the best profit – not a cheap market.

A price might be differentiated by time – for example, launch a third generation mobile phone – the product will in the short term sell for a high price which includes a premium from early adopters. The company will plan to drop the price later until an attack can be launched on the commodity market with the aid of low costs, even including outsourcing.

Some companies might differentiate a product by sector; for example, Toyota have Lexus, Toyota and Daihatsu brands; VAG have Audi, Volkswagen, Seat and Skoda. How much does higher price actually reflect superior quality? Another strategy is to aim for the premium sector for example, make-up or perfume, since people think some products are better if they cost more. Prices might be segregated geographically – for example, pounds sterling, dollars and euros. If you buy a computer in the UK it normally costs more than in the US.

Special order – accept or reject

Sometimes it makes sense to accept a special order even though the price is lower than you would normally charge. This is because the capacity is there anyway – for example you intend to retain your employees even if there is no work for them to do.

EXAMPLE

A double glazing manufacturer is approached by a factory owner who asks for new glazing for a building, at specially low rates. If this is the low season for sales, the manufacturer might be willing to fulfil the order if employees are otherwise under-employed.

Considerations:

- Will the normal market be affected?
- Will all additional (marginal) costs be well covered? These costs are likely to be materials, etc. rather than labour costs since these will have to be paid in any case.
- Is there any risk that the job will overrun or consume scarce resources thus displacing work at normal margins?
- Could the special order lead to other (more profitable) work in the future?
- Could the special order deprive a competitor of a profitable opportunity?

Examples are airline seats and hotel rooms, because the service expires at a given time and **marginal costs** are minimal.

EXAMPLE   Special order – accept or reject

An airport parking facility normally charges £50 per week for a car parking space in its secure facility. Of this charge, £12 is variable cost for hourly paid employees, communications cost and so on. A further £15 is for fixed costs associated with running the facility – annual costs have been divided by the estimated volume of sales to arrive at this figure. A nearby hotel wishes to offer a package to airline passengers of one night's stay at the hotel to include either one, or two weeks' parking. The proposal is that the hotel should enter into partnership with the parking facility, paying £20 per week per car space.

On the face of it this deal does not appear to be a very good one for the car park since the offered price is only 40% of the normal price. However, the deal does offer a positive contribution per space per week of £8 (£20 less £12 variable cost). Fixed costs are ignored. The deal may be worth accepting (especially as administration costs are likely to be lower than for normal sales) as long as there is spare capacity. If the partnership with the hotel were to mean that normal business had to be turned away for lack of space, or direct bookings were lost to the hotel arrangement, then the arrangement should be terminated.

Customer profitability segmentation

Divide your customers up into segments and determine the profitability of each. For example higher-spending customers might be specially approached with mailshots offering financial services; banks have different bank accounts and credit cards for different sectors of their markets.

A leading supermarket sells own-brand lasagne in 'value', plain, colourful and 'special' boxes. The most expensive may cost 300% more than the cheapest.

Focus on more profitable customers and neglect the less profitable ones. Mortgage lenders are believed to 'red-line' some districts, assuming that the small size of loans and the perceived high risk of default make the prospective profit negligible.

Taking it **FURTHER**

In the context of for-profit organisations the assumption is made that the goal of decision making is the maximisation of profit. Even in this sector, things cannot be so simple – how do you evaluate alternatives for expenditure to improve health and safety among employees? In the public sector, social and political factors may predominate. Hospital administrators, for example, face decisions on the best way to maximise the use of scarce resources every day.

Textbook Guide

ATRILL AND MCLANEY: *Chapter 5*
COOMBS ET AL.: *Chapter 8*
DRURY: *Chapters 11, 26*
HORNGREN ET AL.: *Chapter 6*
UPCHURCH: *Chapters 6, 7, 8, 9*
WEETMAN: *Chapter 21*

4	
investment	

Firms sometimes need to consider large investments where the costs and the benefits can be spread over a long period of time. A long term project is generally regarded as one lasting more than a year.

It is not always obvious which costs are relevant to a decision.

Once the relevant costs are identified, it is necessary to quantify them (that is, it is not enough to say that wages are relevant to a decision; it is necessary also to say how much the wages will amount to). There are some complications here: for example, if the project under consideration will last a long time, inflation may be important.

Benefits can be even harder to judge. There is usually a main element which forms the major justification for the investment, but forecasting the exact amount and timing of all income or savings may be impossible.

Usually there will be a single initial investment. Then over the following few years, there will be net cash inflows. Note that while this pattern of initial investment (cash outflow) followed by cash inflows is the normal pattern, there might instead be further outlays at various stages of the project, and at the end there might be receipts from the sale of equipment, for example.

Clearly, as a minimum, the firm will aim to make a profit on each project it invests in.

It is not enough simply to subtract the expected outlay from the expected income and go ahead with any project which gives an answer greater than zero. This approach takes no account of the timing of flows or the cost of money, and if funds are limited and there are several candidates for investment you need a method of choosing between them. Thus, sensible methods of investment appraisal try to quantify the outcomes of projects in various ways.

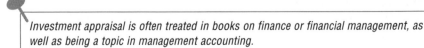

Investment appraisal is often treated in books on finance or financial management, as well as being a topic in management accounting.

EXAMPLE

A project, 'Paris', requires initial investment of £350,000 and produces cash flows over the next five years as follows:

Year	£000s
0	−350
1	60
2	90
3	120
4	200
5	100

We shall look at various methods of evaluating this project.

Conventionally each cash inflow or outflow is regarded as occurring at the end of a year. In the table above there is a cash inflow at the end of year 1 of £60,000, for example. So what does the year zero mean? Since the end of one year is separated from the beginning of the next by only a moment, the end of year 0 is the same as the beginning of year 1. This often represents the time when the initial investment is made, as in the example above.

Accounting rate of return (ARR)

The simplest way is perhaps the most obvious to an accountant: calculating the **accounting rate of return (ARR)** arising from the project. The profit is calculated as a rate of return on the initial investment; a project with an adequate rate of return will go ahead, and if there are competing projects, the one with the highest return will be selected.

In this case we have (in £000s):

Income (60 + 90 + 120 + 200 + 100)/5 = 570/5 = 114 per year
Depreciation (straight-line basis) is 350/5 = 70 per year
Average annual profit = 114 − 70 = 44

The average investment is 350/2 = 175
The accounting rate of return is 44/175 = 25.1%

This method is not entirely satisfactory. One objection is that it takes no account of the timing of flows (a project with all the income in the fifth year would score as highly as one with all the income in the first year) and another is that it does not discriminate between projects of different sizes. The accounting rate of return is not in general use.

Notice that the accounting rate of return method uses profits. All other methods use cash flows exclusively.

With any investment decision, it is important to calculate only the relevant costs. An important difference between the accounting rate of return and the other methods is that only the accounting rate of return includes depreciation. As the other methods are based on cash flows, depreciation is in effect taken into account in the opening expenditure and the proceeds of any disposal at the termination of the project.

Payback

The **payback** method is more widely used, often in conjunction with other methods. It ranks projects solely on how long they take to recover their investment from inflows.

For the 'Paris' project the payback period is 3.4 years – or just under three years and five months. Sometimes it is easy enough to do this 'by eye' but here is a procedure you can follow in more complicated cases. Work from year 0 onwards, calculating a running total until the total becomes positive. This is the fractional year (year 4 below). Take the negative value from the previous year as a proportion of cashflow in the fractional year to find the value of the part-year.

Year	£000s	Cumulative
0	−350	−350
1	60	−290
2	90	−200
3	120	−80
4	200	120
5	100	

Here 80/200 = 0.4 so the whole answer is 3.4 years.

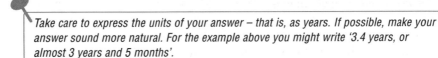

Take care to express the units of your answer – that is, as years. If possible, make your answer sound more natural. For the example above you might write '3.4 years, or almost 3 years and 5 months'.

Payback has defects. It ignores inflows that occur after the investment has been recovered, it does not account for differences in timing before the payback date and it does not distinguish between projects of different sizes.

Nevertheless it is used because of its simplicity and because it implicitly gives a lower value to later inflows, which are both less certain to arrive and of lower value because of the time value of money.

Net present value (NPV)

The *theoretically* favoured methods of evaluation explicitly consider the timing of flows by discounting the cash flows according to the period they fall into. Such methods are referred to as DCF (discounted cash flow) methods. In practice other methods are used, either as an alternative to DCF methods or as confirmation of their results.

Discounting simply means giving a lower value to cash received later. The essence of DCF is that cash received (or paid) in the future is worth less than it is now. The point is that if you receive cash now you can invest it and earn interest.

The first method using DCF involves calculating the **net present value (NPV)** of the flows arising from a project.

Suppose the **discount rate** is 12%. If we invest (say) £50 today, in a year's time our investment will have grown to £56. We can express this as a formula for *future value*:

$$C = PV(1 + r)^t$$

where C is the capital amount, r is the discount rate expressed in decimal form, and t is the number of periods (usually years) for the calculation. Note that this formula assume *compound interest* – the interest earned is reinvested for the next period, unlike *simple interest*. In the case of our £50 investment, after one year it will have grown to

$50(1 + 0.12)^1 = £56$, after 2 years £62.72, and so on.

To calculate the **present value (PV)** of an investment which has a specific value at some point in the future, we can rearrange the formula above:

$$PV = C/(1 + r)^t$$

The present value of £100 received one year in the future at a discount rate of 12% is

$$PV = 100/(1 + 0.12)^1 = £89.29$$

and the value of £100 received after 2 years is

$$PV = 100/(1 + 0.12)^2 = £79.72$$

The NPV approach involves calculating the present value of all the flows arising from a project and taking the net value. A negative NPV would result in a decision not to go ahead, and a positive NPV would result in a decision to undertake the project.

The question arises of how to arrive at the discount rate. If we are using cash that we already have in a bank, the obvious rate would be the interest we are earning at present. This is the opportunity cost of the funds (the amount of the opportunity lost by using the funds to invest in a project).

If we have to borrow the money, the simple approach is to apply the rate we have to pay for the borrowed money, but as we will see later there is a more accurate approach.

When there are several costs or benefits it is convenient to assume that all the flows during a year occur at the end. This makes calculation easier and does not seriously affect the accuracy of the results.

Rather than work out each year's PV from the formula, a table of *discount factors* is often provided. (Note, by the way, that while year 0 has a discount factor of 1, this is not usually shown.) The cashflow is multiplied by the discount factor to give the PV for each year.

Year	£000s	Discount factor (12%)	Present value
0	−350	1.000	−350.0
1	60	0.893	53.6
2	90	0.797	71.7
3	120	0.712	85.4
4	200	0.636	127.2
5	100	0.567	56.7
Total: Net present value			44.6

Adopt some standard layout for your columns and practise it thoroughly. Always include the discount factor column, because you might copy one of the figures down wrongly in an exam but you will be given credit for correct method if it is evident to the examiner what has happened. Also, avoid spurious accuracy – it is ridiculous to calculate NPV to the nearest £1 when the cash flows in the calculation are estimates in any case.

The running themes involved here are clarity and communication – clarity because you will often need to consider only the appropriate facts, and communication because you may have to explain your results to people who are not familiar with the concepts and may expect to see, for example, an allowance for depreciation.

Internal rate of return (IRR)

The alternative method of discounting cash flows is to calculate the **internal rate of return (IRR)**. This is the discount rate which gives an NPV of zero. We might find, for example, that a project has an NPV of £50,000 using a rate of 10%, and that the NPV falls to zero at a rate of 15%. In this case, the IRR is 15%.

The IRR method involves **estimating** the rate of return by finding two adjacent discount rates, one giving a positive NPV and the other a negative NPV, and assuming that the curve joining them is a straight line (whereas it is curved, in reality).

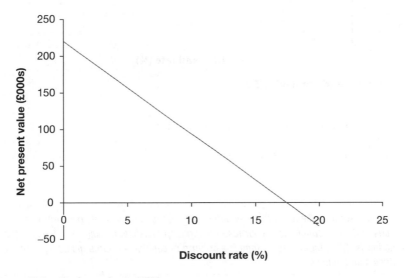

Figure 2.2   Paris project: NPV

We need to focus on the point at which NPV is zero – that is, the point at which the line crosses the X-axis on a chart of NPV for different discount rates. This means choosing one rate with a positive NPV, and an adjacent rate with a negative NPV. For the Paris project our two discount rate 'guesses' might be 16% and 17%. Once we have decided on the two rates, we use tables – or a calculation – to obtain corresponding net present values.

For the Paris project (see p. 38), at 16% the NPV is £3,510 and at 17% it is –£5,630.

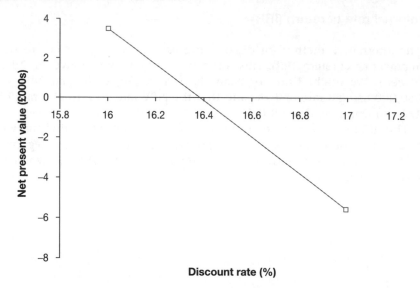

Figure 2.3 Paris project: NPV

Assuming a straight-line function, the IRR is

$16 + 3,510/(3,510 + 5,630) = 16.38\%$

> *You may have to make more than one attempt to home in on suitable discount rates. To practise this, you could check your result using a spreadsheet package – in Excel®, the function is IRR (range) where range is a column of cash flow figures including both outflows and inflows.*

Discounting methods: pros and cons

The NPV method tries to give an accurate measure of the gain to the business from undertaking a project. This is valuable information if indeed and it is available.

The difficulties include that of calculating future cash flows accurately and the danger, the further into the future that we look, of new or changing influences like inflation, political risk, technological change making our calculations completely wrong.

The IRR method does not measure the gain to the business. Instead it calculates a rate of return which, if we are to proceed, should be in excess of the cost of capital.

The difficulties are the same as for the NPV method, and in addition the method does not distinguish accurately between projects. For example, if we use the IRR method we would tend to undertake small projects with a high rate of return rather than much larger projects with a slightly lower rate of return which, because of their size and profitability, would give us a better return.

A further difficulty is that the IRR method assumes that all cash flows within a project are subject to the same rate of return. If the IRR of a particular project is well in excess of the firm's cost of capital, it may not be possible to invest inflows at the IRR rate.

Additionally, it is possible for the IRR method to give more than one answer. In this case it is necessary to make further calculations using NPV to arrive at a decision.

In summary, the NPV method is superior to the IRR method. In practice, where businesses are making investment decisions it is customary to use both NPV and payback.

Exam questions may ask you to comment on the results you obtain, or to comment in general on different methods of investment appraisal. It is worth being familiar with the pros and cons of the four main methods (ARR, payback, NPV and IRR). There is no one ideal method for all circumstances – and no rule to say that only one may be used, either.

Complications

We have worked so far with simple situations and assumptions.

We have assumed that a firm will undertake all projects which pass the appropriate test, whether we choose payback, NPV, IRR or some other hurdle.

However, in the case where there are numerous attractive projects it is by no means certain that there will be sufficient funds available. It may be that the firm would have to borrow, but is unable to raise sufficient funds because of its credit rating; or that it would issue equity but the market is currently unfavourable to such issues. In such cases the firm is subject to hard capital rationing: that is, there is a limit imposed from outside the firm which limits the amount available for capital expenditure.

On the other hand, it might be possible for a firm to raise cash, but for some reason it decides not to do so, perhaps because it regards it as too risky. Where a limit on capital expenditure is self-imposed it is known as soft capital rationing.

Whatever the reason, it may be necessary to choose among several projects, all of which the firm would like to undertake.

It may seem that we can simply select the project with the highest NPV, and then spend whatever is left on the next best project. However, this will not maximise the firm's worth except by accident, because the largest project, requiring most of the available resources, may have the highest NPV.

The appropriate method is to rank the projects by profitability in relation to the investment required (as the funds are the scarce resource in this case). For each project, divide the NPV by the investment to get profitability; rank these results with the highest result indicating the highest-ranking project.

Suppose that the Paris project is in competition for funds with two other projects. We can rank the projects for each method of appraisal:

Year	Paris	Rome	Lisbon
0	−350	−200	−100
1	60	90	30
2	90	80	30
3	120	60	35
4	200	20	40
5	100	20	20
6		10	20
7		10	
Payback period (years)	3.40	2.50	3.13
Ranking	3	1	2
Accounting rate of return	25.1%	12.9%	25.0%
Ranking	1	3	2
Net present value	44.58	20.49	22.52
Ranking	1	3	2
Internal rate of return	16.4%	17.0%	20.0%
Ranking	3	2	1
NPV/investment %	12.7%	10.2%	22.5%
Ranking	2	3	1

On the basis of payback period we would choose Rome; by accounting rate of return and net present value, Paris; by internal rate of return and profitability, Lisbon.

We have previously assumed tacitly that we are making decisions in the absence of inflation, or with an inflation rate of zero. This has been an unrealistic assumption since the 1960s. It is impossible to make correct investment decisions while disregarding inflation, so we need to consider the correct way to deal with it.

The apparent problem caused by inflation is that future cash flows are worth less not only because of the interest effect, but because the money received will be worth less than money being paid out today.

However, that is not really a problem so long as we avoid the traps. There are two of these.

The first trap is that we may neglect to inflate the future cash flows. This is easily done: a saving of £30,000 a year in wages is painstakingly calculated, but clearly this is likely to increase roughly in line with inflation. All future flows are likely to be affected in this way, and this must be accounted for.

The second trap is the result of an attempt to avoid the first trap. It is quite legitimate to express all flows in terms of today's currency, but you must remember that the cost of capital is already expressed in inflated terms, and must be deflated in the same way as future flows.

Expressing future flows in terms of today's money is easy enough: simply do not inflate them.

The real rate of interest (net of inflation) can be calculated simply: we 'sort of' divide the nominal (stated) rate by the inflation rate. The nominal interest rate can be thought of as the real rate increased by applying the inflation rate.

More precisely we can derive the real rate of interest from knowing that a sum of money, P, will grow to $P(1+r)$, where r is the real rate of interest, and to $P(1+r)(1+i)$, where i is the rate of inflation. In this formula r at 5%, for example, is expressed as 0.05.

At times of high inflation, the real rate of interest can be low, or even negative. For example, if you are earning 12% interest on your savings but inflation is running at 10%, your real rate of interest is $(100+12)/(100+10)$ or 1.8%. To make matters worse, you will probably pay tax on the nominal 12% interest paid.

Returning to our topic, then, if we are evaluating a project and using real cash flows, we must calculate the real cost of capital and not use the nominal cost.

There are dangers in this approach, however. One is that different costs will probably inflate at different rates. In the late twentieth century in the UK, labour costs went up faster than prices in general, and costs of computers went down in both nominal and real terms.

Another difficulty is that, as we noted above, tax may well be charged on the nominal returns from the project, so when we come to account for tax in our evaluation we may get it seriously wrong.

Certainly the safest way to deal with inflation is to use money (nominal) cash flows and a money cost of capital.

In this way, the fact that the money we receive in the future is worth less than today's currency is taken care of by the fact that we are using a high rate of interest to discount it.

> *We have seen that we should use either (1) non-inflated (real) cash flows paired with the real (deflated) interest rate, or (2) inflated cash flows paired with the inflated (nominal) interest rate. Never mix the pairs. In numerical exam questions you don't usually get enough information to get it wrong in any case, but if there's a choice, pair like with like.*

It is not difficult to deal with inflation, but you need to remember the theme of clarity – pick out the relevant numbers and ignore the others. You may also need to connect with the theme of communication – these concepts can confuse many people.

Another complication that arises not only in examinations but also in the real world is taxation. The main effect is to improve the NPV of projects with large early outlays on capital equipment, as accelerated tax allowances increase the return. Taking the Paris example from the preceding table, let us make some assumptions:

- Tax is paid a few months after the end of the accounting year at a rate of 30%.
- There is an allowance for 100% of the amount spent on capital items which can be offset against taxable income.
- The company is making sufficient profits elsewhere to offset allowances and losses.

If we pay tax, the net inflow is reduced by the amount of tax paid. Furthermore, as you can see from the following, the pattern of net receipts and payment is quite different from the pattern without tax. This effect could make a project more or less attractive, changing the ranking of projects relative to one another and perhaps changing the decision about which ones to undertake.

Year	Spent/received	Tax	Net
0	(350)		(350)
1	60	105	165
2	90	(18)	72
3	120	(27)	93
4	200	(36)	164
5	100	(60)	40
6		(30)	(30)
	220	(66)	154

Weighted average cost of capital (WACC)

We said earlier that we could use a company's borrowing rate as an approximation to the correct discount rate, and that is useful as a quick guide. However, it is possible for quoted companies to arrive at a more accurate figure.

The point is that their cost of finance is made up of the interest they pay on borrowed money and the cost of paying dividends on their equity. The appropriate discount rate is calculated by averaging these separate costs, but it is important to weight the average by the value of the separate elements giving a **weighted average cost of capital (WACC)**.

For example, a company has equity with a market capitalisation of £500 million costing 12% and debt with a market capitalisation of £200 million costing 6%. Simply averaging the costs gives an average cost of 9%, but the proper calculation is:

Equity	$500/700 \times 12\% =$	8.57%
Debt	$200/700 \times 6\% =$	1.71%
WACC		10.28%

Outcome audit

It is useful to review capital investment decisions towards the end of a project to see if they worked out in accordance with the original forecasts, and some firms do it.

The major benefit would be as a check on the decision making of the firm, but one reason for the dearth of companies undertaking such reviews is that the decision making individuals and processes will probably have changed considerably during the life of the project, so that the value of the review is low.

Behavioural aspects

One reason for the survival of payback criteria despite more modern and theoretically accurate methods is the way people behave.

There is a tendency for managers to be energetic and aggressive. Such individuals are more likely to progress in an organisation by being active rather than passive, and if they succeed they are likely to move on frequently.

They are likely therefore to be biased in the direction of undertaking new projects with benefits due in later years when they are no longer seen as responsible – and may be able to influence decisions by over-stating benefits at the end of a project.

Payback both disqualifies such projects and increases the chances that the initiating manager will still be available to be blamed if a project goes wrong and the benefits fail to materialise.

Taking it **FURTHER**

When we focus on appraisal techniques, the capital investment decision process appears to be an orderly one of obtaining data, presenting calculations and making decisions based on those calculations. In practice, the 'process' is not as tidy as this, since the decisions are important and people are involved. Politics will certainly play a major part. Even the order of events might not be quite what it appears: the investment decision might already have been made by senior management, and the accounting 'ritual' employed to legitimate the decision.

Textbook Guide

ATRILL AND MCLANEY: *Chapter 8*
COOMBS ET AL.: *Chapter 9*
DRURY: *Chapters 13, 14*
HORNGREN ET AL.: *Chapter 11*
UPCHURCH: *Chapters 10, 11*
WEETMAN: *Chapter 25*

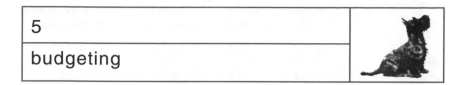

5	
budgeting	

Briefly, a budget is the financial expression of a plan. Most people understand that a budget refers to a one-year plan, as it is futile to plan in detail further than a year ahead. Longer-term plans such as five-year plans are referred to as strategic forecasts or x-year plans.

In any organisation comprising more than a few tens of people, it is necessary to have some form of plan which is communicated to all those responsible for carrying it out. This might simply be an intention to increase sales by 5% in the following year.

Any such plan will have implications for:

- the numbers of salespeople employed;
- the amount of production capacity needed;
- levels of stock to be held;
- borrowing requirements;

to list just a few of the most obvious considerations.

The process of preparing next year's budget usually starts around eight months into the current year. We will assume a financial year starting in January for the purposes of this chapter.

In September we will have a good picture of the actual results for the first two-thirds of the year to the end of August, and of the company's balance sheet at that date. A new forecast for the whole year is prepared which combines actual results to date, with a forecast for the remainder of the year. This forecast is based on the four months' original budget, adjusted for experience of the relationship between budget and actual for the eight months of the year so far. To prepare next year's budget we need to forecast the starting position in January, so we use a revised forecast for the last four months (it is common to produce new forecasts once or twice during the year, as results can stray quite a long way from the budget within three or four months).

The final column in the table below represents a finished forecast of the closing balance sheet at the end of December, and therefore of the opening balance sheet beginning of January next year.

	Budget Jan–August	Actual Jan–August	Budget Jan–December	Forecast 12 months to December
	£000s	£000s	£000s	£000s
Sales	500	620	750	900
Costs	300	345	450	520
Profit	200	275	300	380
Balance sheet at end of:	August	August	December	December
Fixed assets	60	62	60	65
Current assets				
Stock	80	105	80	110
Debtors	120	180	120	180
Cash			20	15
Current liabilities				
Trade creditors	45	51	45	55
Overdraft	80	86		
Net current assets	75	148	175	250
Net assets	135	210	235	315
Shareholders' funds	135	210	235	315

The budget pyramid

Only in the very smallest organisation will a single budget cover all aspects of operations. Normally, the budget is broken down into parts and can be visualised as a pyramid, with detailed budgets at the bottom. These build up to the topmost budget which shows budgeted profit for the entire organisation. If everything goes according to plan, then the overall profit will be achieved. In practice this is highly unlikely, though an under-achievement in one area might be cancelled out by an over-achievement in another area. The whole thing is a balancing act – everyone knows that actual results will differ in detail from the plan, but hopes that overall, results will be on target.

Detailed budgets might be based on function – production or distribution, for example – or reflect some other aspect of the company's organisation, such as divisions by product or geography.

Remember that the budgeted profit for the whole organisation is a very important figure, especially for a quoted company making profit forecasts. This means that despite appearances, the budget-setting process involves a good deal of top-down direction and negotiation.

Budgeting and control

Budgeting is necessary for financial control. Other elements are also affected – for example, plans for sales/production volume could affect logistical requirements (such as warehousing and transport); staffing levels; purchases of capital equipment and insurance requirements. A budget sets the scene for the period in question.

Individuals, even whole teams and departments, may have their performance assessed in part by how well they perform against budget.

The use of budgets for performance assessment means that the budget is not only a tool for communication, but also for control of behaviour. In this sense, it is a political process.

A manager will be responsible for a specific budget (be a 'budget holder'). The budget might cover costs alone, or extend further to revenues and therefore profit. A wider form of 'responsibility centre' is the investment centre in which the manager has authority to buy capital goods.

Obviously it is not satisfactory to hold people responsible for something over which they have no control. This is the principle of 'controllability' under which costs appear in the budgets of those in a position to manage them. In practice it is not always easy to ensure that the principle is observed. For example, a facility may be shared between two departments. Central costs may be allocated between budgets – cleaning, for example – but the managers of these departments may have little control over cleaning expenditure and may not regard the allocation as fair. In theory these costs should not appear at all on the budgets of these departments – if they do, the superior who assesses performance should remember that these costs are not controlled by the departmental manager.

Budget slack

Profit is maximised by setting challenging targets which stretch managers. However the more challenging the target, the more difficulty the manager will face in trying to achieve it, making good performance harder to demonstrate. Therefore there is a tension in the budget setting process. It is in the interests of managers to make the targets as reasonable as possible, by building in some 'slack' so that when things go wrong there is a little room for manoeuvre. Their superiors know this, indeed expect this, and so will set the budgets a little harder than the level they know to be attainable. In response, the managers build in a little extra slack.

Compare the budget negotiation process to bargaining for a purchase in a bazaar – the vendor sets the price too high, and the purchaser makes an initial low offer, and both know they will probably strike a bargain somewhere in between.

Zero-based budgeting

The idea here is to construct budgets without reference to previous budgets. Normally budgets are prepared (at least partly) on the basis of previous budgets rather than being started from scratch and this is known as incremental budgeting. This can result in budget creep in which cost budgets, particularly for overheads, can increase year on year without sufficient scrutiny. In **zero-based budgeting** a case should be made for each cost before it is allowed. In practice the basis is more likely to be the previous year's level than zero. Also, since the procedure is very time-consuming, it might be carried out at intervals, for example every five years.

The cash budget

The **cash budget** is especially important because liquidity is a crucial constraint on a company's activities. Moreover, if funds have to be raised to cover a short term deficit, it will be vital to make the arrangements in advance. In fact the cash budget may itself limit operations – the firm could be in a position to expand but lack the cash resources to meet projected needs such as increased purchases and stocks which will lead to larger creditor payments a short while later. If the firm goes ahead anyway it is 'overtrading' and could collapse altogether because suppliers cease to deliver if they are not paid and if staff are not paid on time they will leave.

EXAMPLE

A toy importer sells directly to retailers. Just before Christmas sales rise markedly and stocks build up. Terms are 60 days for customers and 30 days for suppliers. Temporary staff are employed in warehousing and despatch for the busy period.

	September £000s	October £000s	November £000s
Sales	500	700	1100
Cost of sales			
Opening stock	100	250	500
Purchases	400	600	500
Closing stock	250	500	450
	250	350	550
Gross profit	250	350	550
Wages and salaries	50	70	100
Other costs	100	100	100
Net profit	100	180	350
Cash budget			
Opening balance	50	150	80
Revenue:			
Cash from debtors	500	500	500
Expenditure:			
Payments to creditors	250	400	600
Wages and salaries	50	70	100
Other costs	100	100	100
Cash inflow/outflow	100	−70	−300
Closing balance	150	80	−220

The total profit for the three months is £630,000, but the cash position has worsened from a positive bank balance of £50,000 to an overdraft of £22,0000, a change of £270,000. In total we have an adverse movement of £900,000 to explain.

Debtors have been paying 60 days after the invoice date, which means that cash has not yet been received for October and November sales. Total sales are £2,300,000 and cash from debtors in the three months is £1,500,000. The difference is £800,000.

Creditors are paid 30 days in arrears. Purchases are rising, but due to this delay, the firm has only paid cash of £1,250,000 in the three months, on purchases of £1,500,000 – a difference of £250,000. On the other hand cash has been tied up in stocks, which have risen by £350,000. The net difference of £100,000, added to the debtors' difference of £800,000 matches the £900,000 we were seeking to explain.

This example illustrates the importance of the cash budget. Profits and cash changes for a given period rarely match and specific attention to cashflow is vital.

In this case the firm is clearly profitable and should have no difficulty in extending its overdraft provided that it advised its lenders of the need well in advance. Banks are alarmed by a sudden request for cash, not just because it may indicate an underlying problem but also because it casts doubt on the competence of the firm's management.

The relationship between cash flow and profit is an important theme in accounting. Can you see parallels with the everyday life of individuals? Can you see how an organisation might be cash-rich but making losses?

Tax and VAT

Just as the timing of payments from debtors and payments to creditors is important, so the timing of other payments needs to be taken into account when constructing a cash budget.

VAT does not appear in the profit and loss account for a VAT-registered concern, but it does affect cash flow since the VAT collected on sales (less VAT paid on expenses and so on) is periodically paid to Customs and Excise, typically quarterly.

In the same way other amounts collected on behalf of the government, such as National Insurance and income taxes, are paid monthly. Corporation tax owed by the firm on its profits will also be paid periodically and should also appear in the cash budget.

Taking it ***FURTHER***

If you have not yet been involved in a large-scale budget exercise in the real world, you will probably be surprised by the pressure exerted by personal factors – the organisation is not simply a numbers machine. Perhaps this is right, since the kind of budgets we have been looking at are the financial aspects of a much wider planning process, based on the organisation's mission, strategy and detailed objectives. Financial budgets serve as a focus for communication, are a co-ordinating mechanism and also provide the means of monitoring performance.

Textbook Guide

6
standard costing

Financial reporting tells us how much profit or loss we have made in a period. Comparison with the budget will tell us whether we have surpassed budget or fallen short.

For effective control of operations, we need much more information than that. We need to know how we have performed against our expected costs for each type of item we produce.

Standard costing is a method of setting targets and reporting divergences from them. The main ideas were noted in Chapter 2.

It is necessary in the first place to establish suitable targets. This can be done theoretically, but it will be found that in practice such targets can be less accurate than required. Therefore targets are revised once an item goes into production, and may be revised at intervals as costs and methods change.

The implication here is that standard costing is most useful for environments where large numbers of a particular item are produced, typically manufacturing. In such an environment careful monitoring and control of variable costs can pay large dividends in terms of profit; and the variety of reasons for divergence from standard costs means that we need a formal system of analysis.

There is no reason in theory why standard costing could not be applied in an organisation supplying standardised services in high volumes. However, typically variable costs are small compared with fixed costs so a formal system may cost more than it is worth.

Standards are set on the basis of realistic expectations, not best or worst cases, and they also rely on assumptions about the level of production – usually a level at which there is little idle capacity.

A typical standard will break down the components of a product into its material and processing costs in some detail. A typical cost card was shown earlier.

Periodically the actual outcome will be analysed and **variances** noted.

We will examine an example in some depth, but the first point to note is that the causes of deviation from the expected profit are categorised in such a way as to make corrective action possible. A simple calculation of overall gain or loss against budget would not be very useful.

Flexing budgets

Budgets are prepared at some particular point in time, before the start of the period to which they relate. The level of activity during the period – how many items will be manufactured or how many customers will be served – cannot be known for certain and is estimated. This estimate will be based on a forecast or target and is set to fit in with other elements of the budget for the whole enterprise.

After the end of the period, actual results will be compared in detail with the budget.

Some of the differences will result from a difference in the actual activity level from the estimated level. Others will be due to differences in unit cost, for example in the cost of one kilo of materials or one hour of labour time.

A straightforward comparison between budget and results will tell us nothing about which differences (variances) are differences in activity level (*volume* variances) and which are due to differences in unit cost (*cost* variances). A *variance analysis* is carried out to break the variances down into more detail, distinguishing between production volume and cost variances. Similarly, if the budget includes revenue, the difference between budget and actual revenue can be broken down into two parts. One set of variances result from more or less activity than planned, and the other set result from charging more or less than planned for goods or services.

How can all this be achieved? The key is to flex the budget. The **flexed budget** is created by recalculating the original budget using the actual level of activity. This removes activity variances so they can be dealt with separately. So we end up with three statements: the original budget, the flexed budget, and the actual results.

> It helps to think about when these statements are prepared. The original budget (which will often be referred to simply as 'the budget') will have been prepared before the period in question. The flexed budget is prepared once actual results are known. Indeed it can only prepared then – how else would you know the activity level for which it should be flexed?

Calculating variances

It is easy to get confused by the many types of variance, and pointless trying to learn them by rote. Remember that there are many potentially useful variances; some are frequently used and it certainly helps to recognise these. But the result of a calculation is useful even if you don't actually give the variance a recognised name.

> Think: what am I trying to achieve with this variance? Am I looking at differences in quantity (of materials used, for example) or differences in price?

For variances in materials used in manufacture it is customary to use the expressions 'price' and 'quantity'. For variances associated with labour – such as hourly rate and hours worked – it is customary to use the expressions 'rate' and 'efficiency'. But the arithmetic is identical.

EXAMPLE   Paper boxes

A very simple product is made up from cardboard shapes by hand. The worker who makes the boxes is paid by the hour. When the budget was drawn up for January, the target activity level was set at 3,600 boxes. At the end of January, the actual results are compared with the budget cost.

	Budget			Actual			Variance
	Quantity/ Hours	Price/ Rate	Total cost	Quantity/ Hours	Price/ Rate	Total cost	
Boxes							
Number of finished boxes	3,600			3,450			
Paper shapes							
Number of shapes	3,600			3,450			
Cost per shape		0.40	1,440.00		0.42	1,449.00	9.00
Labour							
Hours @ 60 units per hour	60			56			
Rate of pay per hour		5.00	300.00		5.20	291.20	–8.80
Total			1,740.00			1,740.20	0.20

At first sight, the result seems to be acceptable since the actual cost is almost identical to the budget cost. The materials have cost a little more and the labour has cost a little less, but the overall effect is very close to the estimate. However, further analysis shows that there are, in fact, adverse variances. The first step is to replace the original budget with a flexed budget. This is calculated as if an activity level of 3,450 units had been forecast in the first place. By convention, we label favourable variances 'F' and adverse variances 'A'. Some prefer to use brackets for adverse variances and omit them for favourable ones.

	Flexed			Actual			Variance
	Quantity/ Hours	Price/ Rate	Total cost	Quantity/ Hours	Price/ Rate	Total cost	
Boxes							
Number of finished boxes	3,450			3,450			
Paper shapes							
Number of shapes	3,450			3,450			

Cost per shape	0.40	1,380.00		0.42	1,449.00	69.00 A
Labour						
Hours @ 60						
boxes per hour 57.5			56			
Rate of pay						
per hour	5.00	287.50		5.20	291.20	3.70 A
Total		1,667.50			1,740.20	72.70 A

Now we can see the situation more clearly. The paper shapes have cost more per unit than planned. The labour rate per hour has increased, but this effect has been partly offset by greater efficiency – the boxes have been made in slightly fewer hours than the standard. Overall, the boxes have cost £72.70 more than expected. We can go further in our detective work to find out what happened.

Usage (efficiency) variances

The number of cardboard shapes used (3,450) is exactly the number of shapes which should have been used – there was no waste.

However, we would have expected the production level of 3,450 boxes to take 57.5 hours to complete (this is 3,450/60 units = 57.5). In fact production took 56 hours – a favourable outcome. We can calculate the financial effect exactly; the standard labour rate is £5.00 per hour so the variance is 1.5 hours at £5 per hour which comes to a *favourable* variance of £7.50. Note that we tend to use slightly different terms for labour and materials – the price is called a labour *rate* (not price) and the **usage variance** is called an **efficiency variance**.

Price (rate) variances

The cardboard shapes were expected to cost 40 pence each but actually cost 42 pence each. The **price variance** is:

(0.42 – 0.40) × 3,450 = an adverse variance of £69.00.

What if the prices or rates had not been given per unit or per hour? This does not pose a problem – we still can work out the variances via total cost – but if we want to explain the price changes in terms of one unit or one hour, we will have to use the average.

The labour rate was expected to be £5.00 per hour but was actually £5.20 per hour.

56 hours were worked so the **rate variance** *is*
56 × (5.20 − 5.00) = £11.20 adverse.

We can check our workings; the sum of the individual variances should equal the overall adverse variance of 72.70.

Materials		
Usage	*0*	
Price	*69.00*	
		69.00
Labour		
Efficiency	*7.50*	
Rate	*−11.20*	
		−3.70
Total		*−72.70*

If you have the time, always carry out this check. In an exam you might not have the time to find your error, but you can add a note explaining what you know the total should be. At least this shows that you understand what you are doing!

Variable overheads

Variances relating to those costs which are in some way variable with volume of activity can be analysed in a familiar way, though the terminology is slightly different. Variable *expenditure* variance and variable *efficiency* variance add up to total variable overhead variance. The calculation is identical to the usage and price variances above.

Fixed costs

Fixed costs, of course, are not linked with volume of activity – by definition. However the amount expended may vary from budget and this needs to be taken into account somehow if actual profit is to be reconciled with budgeted profit. It is legitimate to simply state the under- or over-expenditure as a total variance. Alternatively, this total variance can be broken down into two components, the volume and budget variances. The volume variance arises when the actual level of activity differs from the level assumed in the original budget. The budget variance arises when the actual cost differs from the cost justified by the actual level of activity.

Revenue variances

Revenue can differ from budget for various reasons. For standard costing purposes, we say that sales in volume terms may vary from budget or the prices charged may be different, or both. As we did for costs, these differences can be calculated and the terminology is that the sales (margin) volume variance and the sales price variance add up to the total sales variance.

Sales mix

Profit can also vary because the **sales mix** is different from planned – products are sold in different proportions than planned. If the products have differing sales margins, this will make a difference to the profit.

	A	*B*
Budgeted		
Selling price	*10*	*8*
Standard cost	*6*	*5*
Volume	*5,000*	*3,000*
Margin	*4*	*3*
Actual		
Selling price	*10*	*8*
Standard cost	*6*	*5*
Volume	*4,000*	*4,000*
Margin	*4*	*3*

	A	*B*	*Total*
Margin (budgeted)	*20,000*	*9,000*	*29,000*
Margin (actual)	*16,000*	*12,000*	*28,000*

The results show that the actual margin was £1,000 less than budgeted, because of the sales mix – 1,000 units of product B have replaced 1,000 units of product A, but the sales margin on product B is £1 lower.

Reconciling profit

We need to reconcile actual and budgeted profit for several reasons.

An underlying reason for using a standard costing system is to improve control; someone will be required to account for any shortfall in budgeted profit and will need to know the details of what happened.

It is equally important to analyse what happened when we surpass the budget – again to control the system and, where appropriate, to recognise and reward success.

Every significant variation from the budget feeds back into the budget-setting process, letting us know how well our process works. If large variances recur, we may need to recognise that the environment has changed and we need a new forecast for the rest of the year; a quoted company may need to issue a profit warning or update, and any firm must be alive to the dangers outlined earlier of missing its cash forecast.

If we keep finding large fluctuations in variances, we may need to rethink our budget making process for the next year.

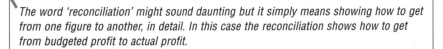

The word 'reconciliation' might sound daunting but it simply means showing how to get from one figure to another, in detail. In this case the reconciliation shows how to get from budgeted profit to actual profit.

EXAMPLE

A company produces a product for which the standard costs are shown below. For January, the planned level of production is 5,000 units. Annual budgeted fixed overheads are £600,000.

	Unit	£s Price/rate	Standard usage	£s Total
Direct materials				
A	kg	5.00	0.5	2.50
B	kg	2.00	1	2.00
Direct labour	hrs	6.00	1	6.00
Variable overheads	hrs	4.00	1	4.00
Standard contribution margin				16.50
Standard selling price				31.00

Actual results for January were as follows:

	Units	Price/Cost	Total
Sales revenue	5,500	30.50	167,750
Direct materials			
A	2,800	4.90	13,720
B	5,400	2.10	11,340
Direct labour	5,450	6.30	34,335
Variable overheads			24,000
Fixed overheads			48,500

The budget is flexed:

	Budget		Actual	
	Original	Flexed	January	Variance
Monthly sales and production	5,000	5,500	5,500	
Sales revenue	155,000	170,500	167,750	−2,750
Direct material A	12,500	13,750	13,720	30
Direct material B	10,000	11,000	11,340	−340
Direct labour	30,000	33,000	34,335	−1,335
Variable overheads	20,000	22,000	24,000	−2,000
Contribution	82,500	90,750	84,355	−6,395
Fixed overheads	50,000	55,000	48,500	6,500
Profit	32,500	35,750	35,855	105

And the variances can be calculated in more detail. Note that the totals should correspond – for example, for material A the two variances below are +280 and −250, totalling +30 to match the table above.

		Original	Standard	January	Variance
Labour hours		5,000	5,500	5,450	
Fixed overhead rate		10.00			
Material A:	price		5.00	4.90	280
	usage		2,750	2,800	−250
Material B:	price		2.00	2.10	−540
	usage		5,500	5,400	200
Direct labour:	rate		6.00	6.30	−1,635
	efficiency				300
Variable overhead:	spending		4.00	24,000	−2,200
	efficiency				200
Fixed overhead:	spending		50,000	48,500	1,500
	efficiency				500
	capacity				4,500

Sales margin variances:

	Original	January
Volume (units)	5,000	5,500
Price	31.00	30.50
Standard contribution	16.50	
Price variance		−2,750
Volume variance (standard costing basis)		8,250

Finally a report can be prepared if required, which reconciles budgeted profit with actual profit.

Budgeted net profit				*32,500*
Sales margin:	*price*	*−2,750*		
	volume	*8,250*	*5,500*	
Direct material:	*price*	*−260*		
	volume	*−50*	*−310*	
Direct labour:	*rate*	*−1,635*		
	efficiency	*300*	*−1,335*	
Fixed overhead:	*expenditure*	*1,500*		
Variable overhead:	*expenditure*	*−2,200*		
	efficiency	*200*	*−500*	
				3,355
Actual profit				*35,855*

> *Some people like to label variances 'favourable' and 'adverse' rather than just showing them as positive or negative. It really doesn't matter, but pick a style and stick to it if your arithmetic is to work first time.*

Again the running theme of clarity comes into play. If you remember that your standard costs plus your variances must equal the figures you were given to work with, you can hardly go far wrong.

Taking it **FURTHER**

Standard costing forms the basis for most systems used in manufacturing industry, and familiarity with these ideas is essential. In practice, there is no standard set of variances for all occasions. If you understand the fundamentals, then it is easy to calculate new variances that someone thinks may be useful. As a student, you might find this unsettling, but turn it to your advantage – if your method is right, you will be rewarded even if you can't remember the name for some of the variances you calculate. Go back to basics – why wasn't this cost (or revenue) what was expected for the volume of activity? Was it the cost, the selling price, the **product mix** or the use of resources?

Textbook Guide

ATRILL AND MCLANEY: *Chapter 7*
COOMBS ET AL.: *Chapters 6, 7*
DRURY: *Chapters 10, 18, 19*
HORNGREN ET AL.: *Chapter 8*
UPCHURCH: *Chapter 14*
WEETMAN: *Chapter 23*

7	
divisional performance	

As companies increase in size it becomes more difficult and less appropriate for management to control detail at the centre. A common way to devolve management is to create divisions based on product groups. Sometimes the divisions are formally part of the same company and sometimes they are legal entities in their own right but the benefits and drawbacks are the same.

Although it can be beneficial in a large organisation to delegate day-to-day management to lower levels, there can also be problems. Divisions may make some of the same products, and will naturally compete against each other in the market, reducing the profits of the company as a whole.

Divisions will report to the centre, and it will be necessary to measure their performance. This may be done both in absolute terms and in terms of what could be expected in the circumstances in which the particular division finds itself.

	£000s
Sales to outside customers	*1,500*
Transfers to other divisions	*200*
Sales revenue	*1,700*
Variable costs	*700*
Contribution margin	*1,000*
Controllable fixed costs	*400*

Controllable contribution	600
Non-controllable fixed costs	120
Divisional contribution	480
Allocated central expenses	50
Divisional net profit	430

Despite theoretical flaws it is still common to use divisional net profit to evaluate performance.

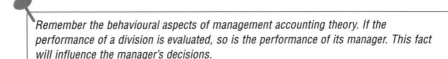

Remember the behavioural aspects of management accounting theory. If the performance of a division is evaluated, so is the performance of its manager. This fact will influence the manager's decisions.

Return on investment

The basis of evaluation is usually **return on investment (ROI)**, as this allows comparison of the performance of units of varying sizes. This is calculated as the return from a project as a percentage of the amount invested.

However, there are difficulties with this approach. Consider the following example. A similar investment is available to the managers of the Paris and Rome divisions. The company cost of capital is 10%. For the company as a whole, projects should be accepted which produce a return in excess of this cost of capital.

	Paris	Rome
	£000s	£000s
Current divisional ROI	8%	14%
Investment	3,000	3,000
Controllable contribution	270	360
Return	9%	12%
Invest?	yes	no

The manager of the Paris division will choose to invest because the return of 9% is better than the division's ROI of 8%. This is not a good decision for the company as a whole since the company cost of capital is 10%. The manager of the Rome division will not accept the project because its return of 12% would reduce the division's overall ROI of 14%. This too is not the best decision for the company as a whole.

Residual income

This is an absolute value, like profit, not a percentage. Divisional income (preferably controllable contribution) is reduced by deducting a charge for the use of assets which is based on the cost of capital.

	Paris	Rome
	£000s	£000s
Investment	3,000	3,000
Controllable contribution	270	360
Charge at 10%	300	300
Residual income	–30	60
Invest?	no	yes

This time the decisions made are in the interest of the company as a whole, as well as of the individual divisions.

Transfer pricing

Transfer pricing is a recurring problem in companies with many divisions. The question arises when one division sells products to another as to what price should be charged.

Typically, a product is transferred in an unfinished state and the receiving division needs to perform further processing before it can be sold to an outside customer. There is therefore no market price for the unfinished (intermediate) product.

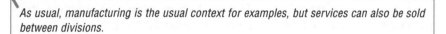

> As usual, manufacturing is the usual context for examples, but services can also be sold between divisions.

There are several ways of setting transfer prices, but there are difficulties with all of them.

Where there is an outside market for the product, the market price serves as an obvious level for internal transfers. There may be a standard discount to reflect cost savings in administration and the absence of a risk premium. In this way the receiving division pays a normal price for the goods and the transferring division has accurate price information to determine whether it can make an acceptable profit.

In the more common case where there is no external market, it is usual to use some kind of formula for simplicity (as many divisions may be transferring large numbers of different products).

It is possible to use marginal cost. Theoretically this optimises decision making in the company as a whole, but will result in the transferring division appearing to be unprofitable, as it will not cover its fixed overheads. In this case, divisional net profit would not be a good way of assessing performance.

Full cost could also be used. Apart from difficulties in assessing full cost, the transferring division will again appear unprofitable.

In practice one of the most popular methods is full cost plus a mark-up. This gives reasonably good information to the transferring division but may lead to sub-optimal decisions by the company as a whole. For example, suppose a division prices a component to another division at cost (£60) plus a mark-up of £40. The buying division can buy externally for £90. If it does so, the company as a whole loses £30, which is the price paid less the internal cost.

It is possible for managers of divisions to negotiate prices among themselves. Given access to appropriate data and the skills to deal with it, this can theoretically optimise the company's decision making. Because of perceived or actual problems, this method is not commonly used. The prices negotiated may depend more on the negotiating skills of the managers involved than on any rational basis, and low transfer prices resulting in low profits may demotivate key workers.

EXAMPLE

Suppose that the Paris division is to make a component which is to be used in a product manufactured by the Lisbon division. Variable costs of the component are £35 and the price for transfer to the Lisbon division is set at £50 on a **cost-plus** basis.

The Lisbon division uses one component per item of its own product and incurs further variable costs of £20 per unit. Market research has shown that the likely sales volumes for the Lisbon product are as follows:

Price (£)	Units
200	1,000
150	3,000
130	5,000
110	7,000

If profit statements are prepared for the Lisbon division, it appears that a selling price of £130 (5,000 units) will produce the best contribution:

Lisbon division

Units	1,000	3,000	5,000	7,000
	£	£	£	£
Price	200	150	130	110
	£000s	£000s	£000s	£000s
Revenue	200	450	650	770
Variable cost	70	210	350	490
Contribution	130	240	300	280

For the Paris division – since the price is fixed – the more units are sold, the more profit is made so the lower the price, the better, according to market estimates.

However the best price for the company as a whole is £110 (7,000 units). Revenue here is external revenue only, and the variable cost ignores the transfer price and simply takes the total variable cost to the two divisions.

Whole company

Units	1,000	3,000	5,000	7,000
	£000s	£000s	£000s	£000s
Revenue	200	450	650	770
Variable cost	55	165	275	385
Contribution	145	285	375	385

To encourage the manager of the Lisbon division to choose the £100 selling price, the transfer price can be pitched at Paris's variable cost of £35. Obviously in this case the performance of the Paris division should not be evaluated on the basis of internal transactions.

Tax authorities in most countries take a keen interest in transfer pricing, as policies can be used to move profit between countries. Companies have been known to use policies that increase profits in low-tax countries at the expense of profits in high-tax countries. The latter have reacted negatively.

It is therefore necessary for companies to use a method that is generally acceptable to tax authorities. Where there is a market price, that seems appropriate, and where there is not, cost-plus is common. There is still some scope for manipulation.

Almost invariably, companies use the same method for internal transactions as they use in declarations for tax purposes.

The theme of communication is important here, as many of the difficulties managers have in accepting the figures for divisional performance come from misunderstanding the purpose of the methods used.

Taking it **_FURTHER_**

The evaluation of divisional performance can be controversial, as every manager wants to show his or her own division in the best possible light. The method of evaluation can be assumed to have an important effect on managerial decisions and motivation. There are many other factors, however, not least among which is the *style* of evaluation adopted by central management, in which greater or lesser emphasis may be placed on financial performance. The behavioural aspects of divisional performance evaluation are similar in many respects to the behavioural aspects of budgeting.

Textbook Guide

ATRILL AND MCLANEY: *Chapter 10*
COOMBS ET AL.: *Chapter 10*
DRURY: *Chapters 20, 21*
HORNGREN ET AL.: *Chapter 10*
UPCHURCH: *Chapter 15*
WEETMAN: *Chapter 24*

8

special topics

Computer information systems

Computers have been used in business since the 1950s. Because early computers were low-powered but expensive, the most efficient way to use them was to have a single processor centrally located with disk or tape storage, serving a number of remote terminals none of which had any processing power. Users queued for processor time to run their jobs, but even with these limitations the benefits to be gained from using computers in business were considerable.

As power increased and cost fell, the model changed to that with which you will be familiar: each user has a powerful computer on his or her desk and the central server's main task is to manage the storage and retrieval of data.

The increased use of computers means that more data than ever is held on the central server, and sometimes it is held in no other form. Security is therefore a vital concern. Information technology (IT) staff control access to data so that the ability to cause damage deliberately or accidentally is restricted. Where the server is connected to the internet, firewall and anti-virus software will be used as a matter of course. Data is backed up at least once a day, usually to tape, and backups are kept off site.

Common uses of computers in business are material requirements planning (**MRP**), ledgers, payroll, spreadsheets and databases.

MRP is used almost exclusively in manufacturing. Like many software applications, it replaces manual work and allows greater effectiveness by making it possible to process many more transactions and calculations.

- The problem which MRP addresses is that of ensuring that sufficient items are available from stock to allow production to continue without maintaining high quantities of stock as a kind of insurance. Carrying stock is expensive.
- An MRP system contains bills of materials (lists of the parts required) for all items produced, a production schedule showing what is to be produced when, and data about suppliers' lead times – how long it takes material to arrive after it is ordered. Given a list of current stock, such a system can calculate requirements and place orders as necessary to meet production demands.

All firms run software for sales ledger, purchase ledger and nominal ledger. The American usage, which is spreading, is to refer to receivables, payables and general ledger. Thus bad debts become delinquent receivables.

As with MRP, a major benefit of running ledgers on computer rather than by hand is the amount of reporting and analysis that is possible cheaply.

- A sales ledger records sales invoices and receipts. Standard packages allow reporting of any or all transactions, lists of amounts owed split by customer and the age of the debt and special reports such as those debts over a certain amount and also over a certain age. Many packages also allow the easy creation of bespoke reports.

- Purchase ledgers give a similar depth and breadth of reporting to sales ledgers, dealing with purchases invoices and payments.
- Nominal ledgers record all the financial transactions of a company, either directly or by means of import from the sales and purchase ledgers. Again, software allows a high volume of transactions and useful reporting.

It is usual for the ledgers in a manufacturing company to be linked to the MRP system. Often the ledger software is purchased from the same company that supplies the MRP software.

Payroll is always computerised in firms with more than a few employees. As employers have to deal with more and more complex legislation, the number of employees for whom it is possible to run a manual payroll system diminishes constantly. As a consequence of this complexity some quite large firms choose to have their payroll processed by a specialist, using the data entered by the client firm, but the range of payroll software is so large and various that most firms use it on site.

You are probably familiar with spreadsheets. Companies use them to analyse one-off projects, for capital expenditure justifications, cash forecasts, budgets and any number of special requirements. With most ledger software it is possible to download data directly into a spreadsheet, saving considerable time and avoiding the inevitable errors associated with manual data entry.

Database software may underlie any of the applications described above. In addition, database management packages (DBMSs) are commonly used by accountants in industry for recording and analysis of larger volumes of data than can be conveniently be dealt with in a spreadsheet. DBMSs also have advantages in data validation and security.

Job and process costing

Job costing: in some industries products are not standard. Each job is tendered for separately; an example is printing one-off products such as brochures or programmes. It is important to be as accurate as possible in estimating costs to avoid taking on loss-making work – or losing jobs to competitors because the quotation is too high. A particular problem is how to take into account overheads. We have already looked at this problem in the context of ABC accounting.

Process costing: some products are produced as the result of a series of processes and at any given time, there will be some product at each stage of production. To ascertain profit, work in progress (WIP) must be valued as well as finished stock. This involves estimating costs at each stage – including manufacturing overhead. Additionally, as the product is transferred from one process to the next – so that the output from one process is the input to the next – the amount (weight, volume, and so on) may change. For example, there may be evaporation as heat is applied so that the volume decreases. The normal extent of this loss will be known and can be used to calculate expected output.

EXAMPLE

The following data on a product at a particular moment in time is available:

Opening WIP	3,000
Materials – average state of completion	35%
Materials – cost	8,000
Labour and overheads – completion	25%
Lab and overheads	5,000
Completed and transferred to next process	12,000
Closing WIP	3,500
Materials – average state of completion	75%
Labour and overheads – completion	30%
Costs added during period	
Materials	36,000
Labour and overheads	50,000

The cost of the product can now be calculated:

Units to be accounted for	
Opening WIP	3,000
Produced entirely within period	9,000
Units transferred	12,000
Closing WIP	3,500
Total units in the system	15,500

Units –	Total	Materials	Labour/Overheads
Started and finished in the period	9,000	9,000	9,000
Completion of opening WIP			
Finished less starting % × opening WIP	3,000	1,950	2,250
Starting closing WIP	3,500	2,625	1,050
Totals	15,500	13,575	12,300

Costs incurred		86,000	
Costs brought forward		13,000	
Total		99,000	
Costs per unit		36,000	50,000
Equivalent units as above		13,575	12,300
Cost per unit	6.72	2.65	4.07

Value of units transferred to next process:

Costs brought forward			13,000
Finishing opening WIP:			
	Units	£	
Materials	1,950	2.65	5,171
Labour and overheads	2,250	4.07	9,146
Total			14,318
New units started and finished	9,000	6.72	60,453
Total			87,770
Closing WIP			
Materials	2,625	2.65	6,961
Labour and overheads	1,050	4.07	4,268
Total			11,230
Total costs			99,000

Economic order quantity (EOQ)

Stock is often one of the most valuable assets of industrial companies. However, its purchase requires use of the company's cash, thus increasing interest costs. In addition, there are *holding costs*, such as:

- the cost of storage facilities, perhaps in a climate-controlled warehouse;
- the cost of staff to look after the stocks – and maintain stock records; and
- the cost of changes in the status of stock – while it is in the company's possession it can be lost, stolen, damaged or become obsolete.

For these and other reasons, companies try to minimise their stock-holdings subject to the needs of production and sales. It can be expensive to run out of parts during a production run, and if finished goods are not available for sale an order may go to a competitor.

'Just-in-time' (JIT) inventory management is one approach, and if successful will save costs by improving efficiency and passing on working capital costs to suppliers. JIT is not suitable for every situation, however, and where it is not in operation the firm still needs to minimise inventory cost.

If minimising stock were the only concern, firms would hold stock at very low levels and order frequently. However, there are also *order costs* associated with ordering, such as staff costs for:

- preparing and processing a purchase order;
- receiving and storing goods as they arrive; and
- processing purchase invoices and payments.

Frequent, smaller orders may also mean higher delivery charges from the supplier and the loss of discounts for quantity.

It may not be too difficult to determine the volume or *usage* of an item of inventory, which is an estimate of how much is likely to be used over a period of time, such as one year. The problem now is to determine what the *ordering schedule* should be. How often should the item be ordered – and therefore, how much should be ordered at any one time?

We can calculate the optimum order quantity using the expression

$T = DC/Q + QH/2$, where

T = total cost
D = usage for the period
C = the cost of one order
H = the cost of holding one unit of stock

Differentiating with respect to Q and setting the derivative to zero, as we are seeking a minimum, gives the **economic order quantity (EOQ)** formula:

$Q = \sqrt{(2DC/H)}$

The EOQ formula can be used to determine the order quantity, and will have the effect of minimising the combined costs of *holding* and *ordering* inventory. The formula itself is not complex, but it is important to ensure that units are consistent. Usually, the period of time taken is one year. The order or holding cost will be the cost per item, per year.

$$Q = \sqrt{\frac{2 \times annual\ volume \times order\ cost}{holding\ cost}}$$

The answer Q is the optimum quantity of the item which should be ordered at any one time. The number of orders per year can be derived by dividing Q into the annual volume (usage). Interpret the answer sensibly – there is no such thing as a part order, so round up or express a fractional answer as something like '9 or 10 orders a year'. The answer can be expressed as the time interval between orders. Take a year as 365 days and avoid fractional days!

EXAMPLE

A company holds stocks of a product as follows:

Annual usage	*2,000 units*
Cost of placing an order	*£120*
Cost of holding one unit of product for a year	*£12*

Applying the EOQ formula,

Q = square root of (2 × 2,000 × 120) / 12 = square root of 40,000 = 200 units
2,000/200 = 10 times a year or about once every 36 days

What does this optimised schedule mean for the firm?

The ordering cost will be (10 × 120) = £1,200 per year. The holding cost will be based on an average stockholding of 100 units (minimum zero units, maximum 200 immediately after a delivery).

(100 × 12) = £1,200 holding cost per year

It is no coincidence that these two values are the same. The EOQ is the point at which the ordering cost and the holding cost lines intersect, as can be seen on the chart below.

We can introduce a couple of additional assumptions to make this example more realistic. Suppose that the firm keeps a base stock of 50 units to try and make sure that the item is never out of stock, even if there are order or delivery delays. Also, suppose that the normal *lead time* for delivery is 14 days (the time between order and delivery). The EOQ and the order cost are unchanged, but the holding cost is higher because an extra 50 units are held in stock:

(150 × 12) = £1,800 holding cost per year

Can the order be triggered by a fall in holdings to a pre-determined level?

During the 14 days' lead time, usage is (2,000 × 14/365) = 77 units. 50 units are always held in stock anyway, so the re-order level is (77 + 50) = 127 units.

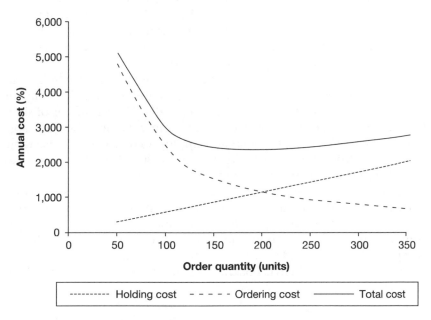

Figure 2.4   Economic order quantity

Competitive advantage

Competitive advantage may arise in several ways, some accidental and some contrived.

Low labour costs are the most widespread competitive advantage because most developing countries go through a phase in which they are able to offer reasonable quality of output while the workforce is still moving from a subsistence basis to a developed country level of consumption.

Low labour costs are often found in areas with cheap or free pollution and health and safety expenditure, as controls tend to follow industrialisation rather than accompany it.

At the same time, new industries may receive direct government help in terms of free or cheap land, financing and so on, as part of an attempt to launch the economy into a more productive level.

Industry may be helped by having a competitive currency, manipulated directly or indirectly by the government.

Government can also help by providing free or cheap, high-quality education. In most countries this is especially advantageous to women, as men tend to receive most of the expensive, scarce education.

Government can also help indirectly by providing sound legal frameworks. Industry works best where there are clear, enforced property laws and transactions can be performed without fiscal drag from bribery and corruption. There are many counter-examples.

As industries grow, they can achieve economies of scale where a company's central costs are spread over larger volumes of output and better rates can be obtained from suppliers. Eventually concentrations of similar companies can form, leading to an environment where there are large numbers of competitors, suppliers and employees with easily transferable skills. While this can make life harder for individual firms, the industry as a whole tends to benefit – the 'Silicon Valley' effect.

Accountants can help by tracking market share and assessing competitors' costs from publicly available data. Competitive advantage arising from technological or product innovation may not last for long as competitors copy innovation, but at least the decision makers in the company can be provided with information which will help them to evaluate the financial effects of their decisions – such as price changes, for example.

Measuring cycle time

In a retail or manufacturing firm, the **operating cycle** usually covers the following events:

1 Take delivery of stock or raw materials.

2 Store it for a while.

3 Perhaps manufacture finished goods.

4 At some point, pay the supplier.

5 Sell it to a customer.

6 Finally the customer pays.

Each type of industry has its own broad type of cycle, and each individual firm has its own characteristics which may even alter the order of events in the cycle. For example a manufacturing firm may operate a just-in-time system, seeking to cut down on step (2); a food retailer might take cash only from customers, while paying suppliers on credit terms so that step (4) comes a long time after receipt of cash and interest on investments is a significant part of profit.

The operating cycle – the whole interval, from step (1) to step (6) – has to be financed by somebody, ideally somebody else (JIT). The cash cycle, from steps (4) to (6), however, must be financed by the firm itself.

The shorter the operating cycle, the less working capital the firm will need. Freeing up working capital improves profit because interest can be earned on cash – or interest saved on borrowings.

To calculate the operating cycle, the time periods are first estimated, probably by averaging over some considerable period of time, such as a year. Now add them all up – except the credit period taken by the firm from suppliers. Now calculate the *cash cycle* by deducting the supplier credit period.

> *Make sure all the time periods are in the same units, such as days or weeks, and include this unit in your answer.*

EXAMPLE

Two companies have an operating cycle as shown below. One is a chain of retail supermarkets and the other is a manufacturing business.

	Weeks	
	A	*B*
Stock turnover	11	1
Production period	3	0
Debtor turnover	6	0
Creditor turnover	6	6

Company A:

The operating cycle is (11 + 3 + 6) = 20 weeks.
The cash cycle is (20 − 6) = 14 weeks.

This must be the manufacturing company, because there is a production period.

Company B:

The operating cycle is 1 week.
The cash cycle is (1 − 6) = −5 weeks (a negative value).

Evidently no credit is allowed to customers.

 Taking it *FURTHER*

Finally ... if a question requires you to write a report for a specific purpose, or to address recommendations to specific people, think about what this means – and show that you can exercise some tact! It makes no sense, for example, to talk vaguely about 'management' if you are addressing the Board of Directors. What level of management are you talking about? Are you describing past actions of your readers in harsh terms or suggesting changes they have no power to bring about?

Textbook Guide

ATRILL AND MCLANEY: *Chapters 9, 11*
DRURY: *Chapters 4, 5, 6, 25*
HORNGREN ET AL.: *Chapters 5, 6, 13, 14,*
UPCHURCH: *Chapter 2*
WEETMAN: *Chapters 19, 20, 21, 26*

part three*
study, writing and revision skills

This part is designed to help you profit from your lectures, benefit from your seminars, construct your essays efficiently, develop effective revision strategies and respond comprehensively to the pressures of exam situations. In the five sections that lie ahead you will be presented with: checklists and bullet points to focus your attention on key issues; exercises to help you participate actively in the learning experience; illustrations and analogies to enable you to anchor learning principles in every day events and experiences; worked examples to demonstrate the use of such features as structure, headings and continuity; tips that provide practical advice in nutshell form.

*in collaboration with David McIlroy

1

how to get the most out of your lectures

This section will show you how to:

- Make the most of your lecture notes.
- Prepare your mind for new terms.
- Develop an independent approach to learning.
- Write efficient summary notes from lectures.
- Take the initiative in building on your lectures.

Keeping in context

According to higher educational commentators and advisors, best quality learning is facilitated when it is set within an overall learning context. Such a panoramic view can be achieved by becoming familiar with the outline content of both a given subject and the entire study programme. Before you go into each lecture you should briefly remind yourself of where it fits into the overall scheme of things. The same principle applies to your course – find your way around your study programme and locate the position of each subject and lecture within this overall framework.

Use of lecture notes

It is always beneficial to do some preliminary reading before you enter a lecture. If lecture notes are provided in advance (for example, electronically), then print these out, read over them and bring them with you to the lecture. You can insert question marks on issues where you will need further clarification. Some lecturers prefer to provide full notes, some prefer to make skeleton outlines available and some prefer to issue no notes at all! If notes are provided, take full advantage and supplement these with your own notes as you listen. In a later section on memory techniques you see that humans possess ability for 're-learning savings' – that is, it is easier to learn material the second time round, as it is evident that we have a capacity to hold residual memory deposits. So some basic preparation will equip you with a great advantage – you will be able to 'tune in' and think more clearly about the lecture than you would have done with the preliminary work.

> *If you set yourself too many tedious tasks at the early stages of your academic programme you may lose some motivation and momentum. A series of short, simple, achievable tasks can give your mind the 'lubrication' you need. For example, you are more likely to maintain preliminary reading for a lecture if you set modest targets.*

Mastering technical terms

Let us assume that in an early lecture you are introduced to a series of new terms such as 'paradigm', 'empirical' and 'zeitgeist'. Some subjects require technical terms and the use of them is unavoidable. New words can be threatening, especially if you have to face a string of them in one lecture. The uncertainty about the new terms may impair your ability to benefit fully from the lecture and therefore hinder the quality of your learning. However, when you have heard a term a number of times it will not seem as daunting as it initially was. It is claimed that individuals may have particular strengths in the scope of their vocabulary. Some people may have a good recognition vocabulary – they immediately know what a word means when they read it or hear it in context. Others have a good command of language when they speak – they have an ability to recall words freely. Still others are more fluent in recall when they write – words seem to flow rapidly for them when they engage in the dynamics of writing. You can work at developing all three approaches in your course, and the checklist below the next paragraph may be of some help in mastering and marshalling the terms you hear in lectures.

In terms of learning new words, it will be very useful if you can first try to work out what they mean from their context when you first encounter them. You might be much better at this than you imagine especially if there is only one word in the sentence that you do not understand. It would also be very useful if you could obtain a small indexed notebook and use this to build up your own glossary of terms. In this way you could include a definition of a word, an example of its use, where it fits into a theory and any practical application of it.

Checklist: Mastering terms used in your lectures

✓ Read the lecture notes or outline before the lecture and list any unfamiliar terms.

✓ Read over the listed terms until you are familiar with their sound.

✓ Try to work out meanings of terms from their context.

✓ Write out a sentence that includes the new word (do this for each word).

✓ Meet with other students and test each other with the technical terms.

✓ Jot down new words you hear in lectures and check out the meaning soon afterwards.

Your confidence will greatly increase when you begin to follow the flow of arguments that contain technical terms, and more especially when you can freely use the terms yourself in speaking and writing.

Developing independent study

In the current educational ethos there are the twin aims of cultivating team-work/group activities and independent learning. There is not necessarily a conflict between the two, as they should complement each other. For example, if you are committed to independent learning you have more to offer other students when you work in small groups, and you will also be prompted to follow up on the leads given by them. Furthermore, the guidelines given to you in lectures are designed to lead you into deeper independent study. The issues raised in lectures are pointers to provide direction and structure for your extended personal pursuit. Your aim should invariably be to build on what you are given, and you should never think of merely regurgitating the bare bones of lecture material in a coursework essay or exam.

It is always very refreshing to a marker to be given work from a student that contains recent studies that the examiner had not previously encountered.

Note-taking strategy

Note-taking in lectures is an art that you will only perfect with practice and by trial and error. Each student should find the formula that works best for him or her. What works for one, does not work for the other.

Some students can write more quickly than others, some are better at shorthand than others and some are better at deciphering their own scrawl! The problem will always be to try to find a balance between concentrating beneficially on what you hear, and making sufficient notes that will enable you to comprehend later what you have heard. You should not however become frustrated by the fact that you will not understand or remember immediately everything you have heard.

> *By being present at a lecture, and by making some attempt to attend to what you hear, you will already have a substantial advantage over those students who do not attend.*

Guidelines: Note-taking in lectures

✓ Develop the note-taking strategy that works best for you.

✓ Work at finding a balance between listening and writing.

✓ Make some use of optimal shorthand (for example, a few key words may summarise a story).

✓ Too much writing may impair the flow of the lecture for you.

✓ Too much writing may impair the quality of your notes.

✓ Some limited notes are better than none.

✓ Good note-taking may facilitate deeper processing of information.

✓ It is essential to 'tidy up' notes as soon as possible after a lecture.

✓ Reading over notes soon after lectures will consolidate your learning.

> *Make sure you annotate your notes with the date and subject and whatever other information you need to tie your notes in with the lecture programme when you come to revise. File your notes with earlier notes as soon as you can.*

Developing the lecture

Some educationalists have criticised the value of lectures because they allege that these are a mode of merely 'passive learning'. This can certainly be an accurate conclusion to arrive at (that is, if students approach lectures in the wrong way). But as a student you can ensure that you are not merely a passive recipient of information by taking steps to develop the lecture yourself. A list of suggestions is presented below to help you take the initiative in developing the lecture content.

Checklist: Ensuring that the lecture is not merely a passive experience

✓ Try to interact with the lecture material by asking questions.

✓ Highlight points that you would like to develop in personal study.

✓ Trace connections between the lecture and other parts of your study programme.

✓ Bring together notes from the lecture and other sources.

✓ Restructure the lecture outline into your own preferred format.

✓ Think of ways in which aspects of the lecture material can be applied.

✓ Design ways in which aspects of the lecture material can be illustrated.

✓ If the lecturer invites questions, make a note of all the questions asked.

✓ Follow up on issues of interest that have arisen out of the lecture.

> *You can contribute to this active involvement in a lecture by engaging with the material before, during and after it is delivered.*

2	
# how to make the most of seminars	

This section will show you how to:

- Be aware of the value of seminars.
- Focus on links to learning.
- Recognise qualities you can use repeatedly.
- Manage potential problems in seminars.
- Prepare yourself adequately for seminars.

Not to be underestimated

Seminars are sometimes poorly attended because their value is under-estimated. Some students may be convinced that the lecture is the truly authoritative way to receive quality information. Undoubtedly, lectures play an important role in an academic programme, but seminars have a unique contribution to learning that will complement lectures and if seminars were to be removed from academic programmes, then something really important would be lost.

Checklist: Some useful features of seminars

✓ Can identify problems that you had not thought of.

✓ Can clear up confusing issues.

✓ Allow you to ask questions and make comments.

✓ Can help you develop friendships and teamwork.

✓ Enable you to refresh and consolidate your knowledge.

✓ Can help you sharpen motivation and redirect study efforts.

An asset to complement other learning activities

In higher education at the present time there is emphasis on variety – variety in delivery, learning experience, learning styles and assessment methods. The seminar is deemed to hold an important place within the overall scheme of teaching, learning and assessment. In some programmes the seminars are directly linked to the assessment task. Whether or not they have such a place in your course, they will provide you with a unique opportunity to learn and develop.

In a seminar you will hear a variety of contributions, and different perspectives and emphases. You will have the chance to interrupt and the experience of being interrupted – you will also learn that you can get things wrong and still survive! It is often the case that when one student admits that they did not know some important piece of information, other students quickly follow on to the same admission in the wake of this. If you can learn to ask questions and without worrying about feeling stupid, you will make a valuable contribution to the seminars you attend.

The right climate in seminars

In lectures your main role is to listen and take notes, but in seminars there is the challenge to strike the right balance between listening and speaking. It is important to make a beginning in speaking even if it is just to repeat something that you agree with. You can also learn to disagree in an agreeable way. For example you can raise a question against what someone else has said and pose this in a good tone – for example, 'If that is the case, does that not mean that … '. In addition it is perfectly possible to disagree with others while avoiding personal attacks, such as, 'that was a really stupid thing to say', or 'I thought you knew better than that', or 'I'm surprised that you don't know that by now'. Educationalists say that it is important to have the right climate to learn in, and the avoidance of unnecessary conflict will foster such a climate.

Links in learning and transferable skills

An important principle in learning to progress from shallow to deep learning is developing the capacity to make connecting links between themes or topics and across subjects. This also applies to the various learning activities such as lectures, seminars, fieldwork, computer searches and private study.

Another factor to think about is, 'What skills can I develop, or improve on, from seminars that I can use across my study programme?' Examples of key skills are the ability to communicate and the capacity to work within a team. These are skills that you will be able to use at various points in your course (transferable skills).

Checklist: How to benefit from seminars

✓ Do some preparatory reading.
✓ Familiarise yourself with the main ideas to be addressed.
✓ Make notes during the seminar.
✓ Make some verbal contribution, such as a question.
✓ Remind yourself of the skills you can develop.
✓ Trace learning links from the seminar to other subjects/topics on your programme.
✓ Make brief bullet points on what you should follow up on.
✓ Read over your notes as soon as possible after the seminar.
✓ Continue discussion with fellow students after the seminar has ended.

Checklist: Presentations

✓ Be selective in what you choose to present. The aim of a presentation is to persuade your audience, not lecture them.

✓ Remember that slides are just a visual aid. The slides are not the presentation – your talk is.

✓ Space out points clearly on visuals (large and legible). Don't distract your audience by making them read a lot of text, or they won't hear you.

✓ Map out where you are going (but don't overdo it) and summarise main points at the end.

✓ If you are bringing an electronic presentation (Microsoft® PowerPoint®) bring the file in more than one form for example, on floppy *and* on a USB memory stick drive. Belt *and* braces.

✓ Check out beforehand that you know how the equipment works and work out where you are going to stand so as not to obstruct the audience's view.

✓ Spread eye contact around the audience – especially, do not address your tutor all the time – treat him or her as one of the audience.

✓ Avoid reading out at all costs. If you really must, use cue cards, but only make skeleton notes on them (in big writing). Better to glance at the slide (on projector bed or computer monitor) for cues – but maintain eye contact with your audience almost all the time.

✓ If the slide is projected behind you, resist the temptation to turn round to look at it. You lose contact with the audience and your voice will fade every time you do it.

✓ Time your talk carefully and above all don't run over time. As a rule of thumb, rehearse for a 12 minute talk if you have a 15 minute slot. Of course allow additional time for questions if appropriate.

✓ Make sure your talk synchronises with the slide on view at any given point.

✓ Have a practice run with friends if possible but in any event *rehearse*.

✓ Consider involving your audience by asking *them* questions: 'How many of you ... '. This might also be a useful desperation tactic if you invite questions and no one volunteers.

> *You may well be nervous. This is fine – everyone gets nervous and your audience will understand. But anticipate the effects of nervousness – keep your voice loud enough and keep up eye contact. Remember that if you pause to collect your thoughts, the pause seems a lot longer to you than it does to your audience. So don't panic, pause.*

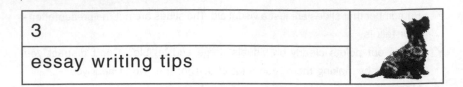

3

essay writing tips

This section will show you how to:

- Quickly engage with the main arguments.
- Channel your passions constructively.
- Note your main arguments in an outline.
- Find and focus on your central topic questions.
- Weave quotations into your essay.

Getting into the flow

In essay writing one of your first aims should be to get your mind active and engaged with your subject. Tennis players like to go out onto the court and hit the ball back and forth just before the competitive match begins. This allows them to judge the bounce of the ball, feel its weight against the racket, get used to the height of the net, the parameters of the court and other factors such as temperature, light, sun and the crowd. In the same way you can 'warm up' for your essay by tossing the ideas to and fro within your head before you begin to write. This will allow you to think within the framework of your topic, and this will be especially important if you are coming to the subject for the first time.

The tributary principle

A tributary is a stream that runs into a main river as it wends its way to the sea. Similarly in an essay you should ensure that every idea you introduce is moving towards the overall theme you are addressing. Your idea might of course be relevant to a subheading that is in turn relevant to a main heading. Every idea you introduce is to be a 'feeder' into the flowing theme. In addition to tributaries, there can also be 'distributaries', which are streams that flow away from the river. In an essay these would represent the ideas that run away from the main stream of thought and leave the reader trying to work out what their relevance may have been. It is one thing to have grasped your subject thoroughly, but quite another to convince your reader that this is the case. Your aim should be to build up ideas sentence-by-sentence and paragraph-by-paragraph, until you have communicated your clear purpose to the reader.

> *It is important in essay writing that you do not only include material that is relevant, but that you also make the linking statements that show the connection to the reader.*

The mind map approach

You will be familiar with this approach, in which the central topic is placed at the centre of a map and relevant concepts are connected to it, and to each other by lines. Some people find this approach really helpful for essay planning and some don't. A major advantage of the mind map is that it is not linear – it doesn't dictate the order in which ideas will be presented in the finished essay. This allows you to add in extra ideas at any time and can also make for a better essay.

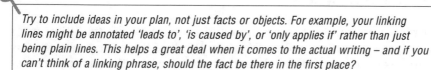

> *Try to include ideas in your plan, not just facts or objects. For example, your linking lines might be annotated 'leads to', 'is caused by', or 'only applies if' rather than just being plain lines. This helps a great deal when it comes to the actual writing – and if you can't think of a linking phrase, should the fact be there in the first place?*

Listing and linking the key concepts

All subjects will have central concepts that can sometimes be usefully labelled by a single word. Course textbooks may include a glossary of terms and these provide a direct route to the beginning of efficient mastery of the topic. The central words or terms are the essential raw materials that you will need to build upon. Ensure that you learn the words and their definitions, and that you can go on to link the key words together so that in your learning activities you will add understanding to your basic memory work.

> *It is useful to list your key words under general headings if that is possible and logical. You may not always see the connections immediately but when you later come back to a problem that seemed intractable, you will often find that your thinking is much clearer.*

EXAMPLE Write an essay on 'Aspects and perceptions of ageing'

You might decide to draft your outline points in the following manner (or you may prefer to use a mind map approach):

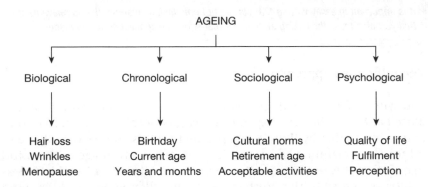

AGEING

Biological	Chronological	Sociological	Psychological
Hair loss	Birthday	Cultural norms	Quality of life
Wrinkles	Current age	Retirement age	Fulfilment
Menopause	Years and months	Acceptable activities	Perception

An adversarial system

In higher education students are required to make the transition from descriptive to critical writing. You can think of the critical approach as being like a court case that is being conducted where there is both a prosecution and a defence. Your concern should be for objectivity, transparency and fairness. No matter how passionately you may feel about a given cause you must not allow information to be filtered out because of your personal prejudice. An essay is not to become a crusade for a cause in which the contrary arguments are not addressed in an evenhanded manner. This means that you should show awareness that opposite views are held and you should at least represent these as accurately as possible.

> *Your role as the writer is like that of the judge in that you must ensure that all the evidence is heard, and that nothing will compromise either party.*

Stirring up passions

The above points do not of course mean that you are not entitled to a personal persuasion or to feel passionately about your subject. On the contrary, such feelings may well be a marked advantage if you can bring them under control and channel them into balanced, effective writing (see example below). Some students may be struggling at the other end of the spectrum – being required to write about a topic that they feel quite indifferent about. As you engage with your topic and toss the ideas around in your mind, you will hopefully find that your interest is stimulated, if only at an intellectual level initially. How strongly you feel about a topic, or how much you are interested in it, may depend on whether you choose the topic yourself or whether it has been given to you as an obligatory assignment.

It is important that in a large project (such as a dissertation) you choose a topic for which you can maintain your motivation, momentum and enthusiasm.

EXAMPLE   An issue that may stir up passions

Arguments for and against the existence of God:

For

- Universe appears to have a design.
- Humans have an innate desire to worship.
- Humans are free to choose good or evil.
- Common threads between religions.
- Religion provides strong moral foundations.
- Individuals report subjective experiences.
- God's revelation is in holy books.

Against

- There are flaws in the universe.
- Not all appear to have the desire to worship.
- How can evil be adequately explained?
- Many religions and diverse beliefs.
- Humanists accept moral principles.
- Subjective experiences not infallible.
- Devout people differ in interpretation.

Structuring an outline

Whenever you sense a flow of inspiration to write on a given subject, it is essential that you put this into a structure that will allow your inspiration to be communicated clearly. It is a basic principle in all walks of life that structure and order facilitate good communication. Therefore, when you have the flow of inspiration in your essay you must get this into a structure that will allow the assessor to recognise the true quality of your work. For example you might plan for an introduction, conclusion, three main headings and each of these with several subheadings (see example below). Moreover, you may decide not to include your headings in your final presentation – just use them initially to structure and balance your arguments. Once you have drafted this outline you can then easily sketch an introduction, and you will have been well prepared for the conclusion when you arrive at that point.

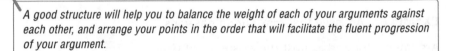

A good structure will help you to balance the weight of each of your arguments against each other, and arrange your points in the order that will facilitate the fluent progression of your argument.

EXAMPLE   **Write an essay that assesses the dynamics of the housing market in the decision to purchase or delay**

(Notice that this plan consists of statements, not just topic headings, and will make the essay much easier to write as a result.)

1 The quest to be on the property ladder:

  a   a house is an investment;
  b   rent payments are a 'black hole' for money;
  c   insufficient quantity of houses for growing needs;
  d   social pressure to be a homeowner.

2 Compounded problems for first time buyers:

  a   delay in purchase to save deposit;
  b   ratio balance of salary against mortgage;
  c   balancing mortgage costs with preferred life-style;
  d   balancing the choice of house with the choice of area.

3 The problem of inflationary pressures:

    a   uncertainty of interest rates and world economies;
    b   income may fall behind inflation;
    c   future house price slumps could create negative equity;
    d   conflicting reports in economic forecasts.

Finding major questions

When you are constructing a draft outline for an essay or project, you should ask what is the major question or questions you wish to address. It would be useful to make a list of all the issues that spring to mind that you might wish to tackle. The ability to design a good question is an art form that should be cultivated, and such questions will allow you to impress your assessor with the quality of your thinking.

> *If you construct your ideas around key questions it will help you focus your mind and engage effectively with your subject. Your role will be like that of a detective – exploring the evidence and investigating the findings.*

To illustrate the point, consider the example presented below. If you were asked to write an essay about the effectiveness of the police in your local community you might, as your starting point, pose the following questions.

EXAMPLE   **The effectiveness of the police in the local community: initial questions**

- Is there a high-profile police presence?
- Are there regular 'on the beat' officers and patrol car activities?
- Do recent statistics show increases or decreases in crime in the area?
- Are the police involved in community activities and local schools?
- Does the local community welcome and support the police?
- Do the police have a good reputation for responding to calls?
- Do the police harass people unnecessarily?
- Do minority groups perceive the police as fair?
- Do the police have an effective complaints procedure to deal with grievances against them?
- Do the police solicit and respond to local community concerns?

Rest your case

It should be your aim to give the clear impression that your arguments are not based entirely on hunches, bias, feelings or intuition. In exam and essay questions it is usually assumed (even if not directly specified) that you will appeal to evidence to support your claims. Therefore, when you write your essay you should ensure that it is liberally sprinkled with citations and evidence. By the time the assessor reaches the end of your work, he or she should be convinced that your conclusions are evidence based. A fatal flaw to be avoided is to make claims for which you have provided no authoritative source. Widespread failure to cite authorities may not be so serious in exam essays, but in coursework will certainly mean an automatic fail.

Give the clear impression that what you have asserted is derived from recognised sources (including up-to-date ones). It also looks impressive if you spread your citations across your essay rather than compressing them into a paragraph or two at the beginning and end.

Citation and referencing

The *citation* is the note embedded in the text, for example, 'Smith (1999)' which allows the reader to look up the list of references at the end of the essay to see details of the Smith article or book.

The *reference* should be complete (get guidelines from your course leader on the approved format in your institution – 'Harvard' style, for example). Don't provide details of the bibliographic database from which you obtained an article electronically (unless specifically asked, of course) – this is irrelevant, since a reader might have access to quite different databases. Instead give full details of the article's appearance in the original journal. References appear in a list of references at the end of the essay. Some people refer to bibliographies, but these are different and consist of a reading list for general interest.

Some examples of how you might introduce your evidence and cite sources are provided below:

According to O'Neil (1999) ...
Wilson (2003) has concluded that ...
Taylor (2004) found that ...
It has been claimed by McKibben (2002) that ...

Appleby (2001) asserted that ...
A review of the evidence by Lawlor (2004) suggests that ...
Findings from a meta-analysis presented by Rea (2003) would indicate that ...

It is sensible to vary the expression used so that you are not monotonous and repetitive, and it also aids variety to introduce researchers' names at various places in the sentence (not always at the beginning). It is advisable to choose the expression that is most appropriate – for example you can make a stronger statement about reviews that have identified recurrent and predominant trends in findings as opposed to one study that appears to run contrary to all the rest.

In terms of referencing, practice may vary from one discipline to the next, but some general points that will go a long way in contributing to good practice are listed below.

Checklist: References

✓ If a reference is cited in the text, it must be in the list at the end (and vice-versa).
✓ Names and dates in text should correspond exactly with the entry in the list of references.
✓ In the Harvard style, the entire references section should be in alphabetical order by the surname (not the initials) of the author or first author.
✓ Any reference you make in the text should be traceable by the reader (they should clearly be able to identify and trace the source).
✓ If you cite a website, locate or invent a name for the website (the name of the company, for example) and include as much information as you can. Don't just type the URL and leave it at that.

Careful use of quotations

Although it is essential to present a good range of cited sources, there is no need to actually present the original author's words as a quotation. Normally, you will present the author's ideas in your own words, with careful citation, of course.

Occasionally you might want to present the original words, and if there is good reason for this (perhaps that author's phrasing has become a recognised name for an idea) then a short quotation is fine. Remember the citation and the full reference.

However, avoid presenting a 'patchwork quilt' – work consisting mainly of pasted together quotations with little thought for interpretative comment or coherent structure. This is not an essay.

Use your evidence and quotations in a manner that demonstrates that you have thought the issues through, and have integrated them in a manner that shows you have been focused and selective in the use of your sources.

A clearly defined introduction

In an introduction to an essay you have the opportunity to define the problem or issue that is being addressed and to set it within context. Resist the temptation to elaborate on any issue at the introductory stage. For example, think of a composer who throws out hints and suggestions of the motifs that the orchestra will later develop. What he or she does in the introduction is to provide little tasters of what will follow in order to whet the audience's appetite. If you go back to the analogy of the game of tennis, you can think of the introduction as marking out the boundaries of the court in which the game is to be played.

If you leave the introduction and definition of your problem until the end of your writing, you will be better placed to map out the directions that will be taken.

Conclusion – adding the finishing touches

In the conclusion you should aim to tie your essay together in a clear and coherent manner. It is your last chance to leave an overall impression in your reader's mind. Therefore, you will at this stage want to do justice to your efforts and not sell yourself short. This is your opportunity to identify where the strongest evidence points or where the balance of probability lies. The conclusion to an exam question often has to be written hurriedly under the pressure of time, but with an essay (coursework) you have time to reflect on, refine and adjust the content to your satisfaction. It should be your goal to make the conclusion a smooth finish that does justice to the range of content in summary and succinct form. Do not underestimate the value of an effective conclusion. 'Sign off' your essay in a manner that brings closure to the treatment of your subject.

The conclusion facilitates the chance to demonstrate where the findings have brought us to date, to highlight the issues that remain unresolved and to point to where future research should take us.

Top-down and bottom-up clarity

An essay gives you the opportunity to refine each sentence and paragraph on your computer. Each sentence is like a tributary that leads into the stream of the paragraph that in turn leads into the mainstream of the essay. From a 'top-down' perspective (namely starting at the top with your major outline points), clarity is facilitated by the structure you draft in your outline. You can ensure that the subheadings are appropriately placed under the most relevant main heading, and that both sub and main headings are arranged in logical sequence. From a 'bottom-up' perspective (namely, building up the details that 'flesh out' your main points), you should check that each sentence is a 'feeder' for the predominant concept in a given paragraph. When all this is done you can check that the transition from one point to the next is smooth rather than abrupt.

Checklist: Summary for essay writing

✓ Before you start, have a 'warm up' by tossing the issues around in your head.

✓ List the major concepts and link them in fluent form.

✓ Design a structure (outline) that will facilitate balance, progression, fluency and clarity.

✓ Pose questions and address these in critical fashion.

✓ Demonstrate that your arguments rest on evidence and spread cited sources across your essay.

✓ Provide an introduction that sets the scene and a conclusion that rounds off the arguments.

4	
revision hints and tips	

This section will show you how to:

- Map out your accumulated material for revision.
- Choose summary tags to guide your revision.
- Keep well-organised folders for revision.
- Make use of effective memory techniques.
- Profit from the benefits of revising with others.
- Attend to the practical exam details that will help keep panic at bay.
- Revise for a management accounting exam.

The return journey

In a return journey you will usually pass by all the same places that you had already passed when you were outward bound. If you had observed the various landmarks on your outward journey your would be likely to remember them on your return. Similarly, revision is a means to 'revisit' what you have encountered before. Familiarity with your material can help reduce anxiety, inspire confidence and fuel motivation for further learning and good performance.

> *If you are to capitalise on your revision period, then you must have your materials arranged and at hand for the time when you are ready to make your 'return journey' through your notes.*

Start at the beginning

Strategy for revision should be on your mind from your first lecture at the beginning of your academic semester. You should be like the squirrel that stores up nuts for the winter. Do not waste any lecture, tutorial, seminar, group discussion, and so on, by letting the material evaporate into thin air. Get into the habit of making a few guidelines for revision after each learning activity. Keep a folder, or file, or little notebook that is reserved for revision and write out the major points that you have learnt. By establishing this regular practice you will find that what you have learnt becomes consolidated in your mind, and you will also be in a better position to 'import' and 'export' your material both within and across subjects.

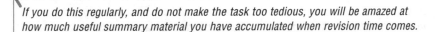

If you do this regularly, and do not make the task too tedious, you will be amazed at how much useful summary material you have accumulated when revision time comes.

Compile summary notes

It would be useful and convenient to have a little notebook or cards on which you can write outline summaries that provide you with an overview of your subject at a glance. You could also use treasury tags to hold different batches of cards together whilst still allowing for inserts and re-sorting. Such practical resources can easily be slipped into your pocket or bag and produced when you are on the bus or train or whilst sitting in a traffic jam. They would also be useful if you are standing in a queue or waiting for someone who is not in a rush! A glance over your notes will consolidate your learning and will also activate your mind to think further about your subject. Therefore it would also be useful to make note of the questions that you would like to think about in greater depth. Your primary task is to get into the habit of constructing outline notes that will be useful for revision, and a worked example is provided below.

There is a part of the mind that will continue to work on problems when you have moved on to focus on other issues. Therefore, if you feed on useful, targeted information, your mind will continue to work on 'automatic pilot' after you have 'switched off'.

Keep organised records

Keep a folder for each subject and divide this topic-by-topic. You can keep your topics in the same order in which they are presented in your course lectures. Bind them together in a ring binder or folder and use subject dividers to keep them apart. Make a numbered list of the contents at the beginning of the folder, and list each topic clearly as it marks a new section in your folder. Another important practice is to place all your notes on a given topic within the appropriate section – don't put off this simple task, do it straightaway. Notes may come from lectures, seminars, tutorials, internet searches, personal notes, and so on. It is also essential that when you remove these for consultation that you return them to their 'home' immediately after use.

> *Academic success has as much to do with good organisation and planning as it has to do with ability. The value of the quality material you have accumulated on your academic programme may be diminished because you have not organised it into an easily retrievable form.*

Use past papers

Revision will be very limited if it is confined to memory work. You should by all means read over your revision cards or notebook and keep the picture of the major facts in front of your mind's eye. It is also, however, essential that you become familiar with previous exam papers so that you will have some idea of how the questions are likely to be framed. Therefore, build up a good range of past exam papers (especially recent ones) and add these to your folder.

EXAMPLE   Using a past question for revision

'Evaluate the pleasures and problems of keeping a pet'. Immediately you can see that you will require two lists and you can begin to work on documenting your reasons under each as below:

Problems

- Vet and food bills.
- Restrictions on holidays/weekends away.
- Friends may not visit.
- Allergies.
- Smells and cleanliness.
- Worries about leaving pet alone.

Pleasures

- Companionship.
- Fun and relaxation.

- Satisfaction from caring.
- Cuddles.
- Contact with other pet owners.
- Good distraction from problems.

You will have also noticed that the word 'evaluate' is in the question – so your mind must go to work on making judgements. You may decide to work through problems first and then through pleasures, or it may be your preference to compare point by point as you go along. Whatever conclusion you come to may be down to personal subjective preference but at least you will have worked through all the issues from both standpoints. The lesson is to ensure that part of your revision should include critical thinking as well as memory work.

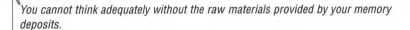

You cannot think adequately without the raw materials provided by your memory deposits.

Employ effective mnemonics (memory aids)

You may well be familiar with these methods from revision at school! They can be helpful to jog your memory and soothe nerves, but are of limited use when you are being assessed on your understanding of a topic, rather than simple (!) retention of facts.

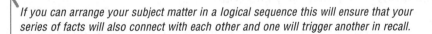

If you can arrange your subject matter in a logical sequence this will ensure that your series of facts will also connect with each other and one will trigger another in recall.

Here are some ideas:

- Acronyms – take the first letter of all the key words and make a word form these. An example from business is SWOT – Strengths, Weaknesses, Opportunities and Threats.
- Rhymes and chimes – words that rhyme and words that end with a similar sound (for example, commemoration, celebration, anticipation). Alliteration is also used – find a set of relevant words that all begin with the same letter.
- Location method – a familiar journey is visualised and you 'place' the facts that you wish to remember at various landmarks along the journey – for example, a bus stop, a car park, a shop, a store, a bend, a police station, a traffic light, and so on. This method is supposedly used by stage memory artists.

- Visualisation – turn information into pictures – the example given about the problems and pleasures of pets could be envisaged as two tug-of-war teams that pull against each other. You could visualise each player as an argument and have the label written on his or her T-shirt.
- Mind maps – they have the advantage of giving you the complete picture at a glance, although they can become a complex work of art! You could carry one around with you, though the main benefit is probably gained from the construction process.

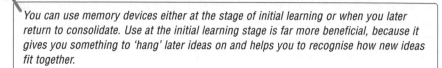

You can use memory devices either at the stage of initial learning or when you later return to consolidate. Use at the initial learning stage is far more beneficial, because it gives you something to 'hang' later ideas on and helps you to recognise how new ideas fit together.

Alternate between revision methods

It is not sufficient to present outline points in response to an exam question (although it is better to do this instead of nothing if you have run out of time in your exam). Your aim should be to put 'meat on the bones' by adding substance, evidence and arguments to your basic points. You should work at finding the balance between the two methods – outline revision cards might be best reserved for short bus journeys, whereas extended reading might be better employed for longer revision slots at home or in the library. Your ultimate goal should be to bring together an effective, working approach that will enable you to face your exam questions comprehensively and confidently.

In revision it is useful to alternate between scanning over your outline points, and reading through your notes, articles, chapters, and so on in an in-depth manner. Also, the use of different times, places and methods will provide you with the variety that might prevent monotony and instead facilitate freshness.

Revising with others

If you can find a few other students to revise with, this will provide another fresh approach to the last stages of your learning. However ensure that others carry their workload and are not merely using the hard work of others as a short cut to success. Having said that – teaching someone else is an excellent method of really learning something!

Before you meet up you can each design some questions for the whole group to address. The group could also go through past exam papers and discuss the points that might provide an effective response to each question.

Checklist: Good study habits for revision time

✓ Set a date for the 'official' beginning of revision and prepare for 'revision mode'.

✓ Do not force cramming by leaving revision too late. You know it makes sense.

✓ Revise in short bursts to avoid saturation.

✓ Take care of your body during the revision season – eat regularly, sleep well, and keep alcohol and caffeine intake to a minimum.

✓ Especially try to keep up your normal level of exercise. Also, stretch and walk round the room regularly during long revision sessions.

Revision for a management accounting examination

- Questions in a management accounting examination usually require a mixture of calculations, and discussion of the results or of the related topic. Sometimes the requirement is framed as a report to a manager or Board of Directors. Revision for the exam therefore needs to include plenty of practice at calculations as well as revision of ideas about the purpose and consequences of management accounting practices.
- Obtain as many past papers as you can, but take more notice of recent papers than old ones. Topics (and examiners' approaches) change over the years. Obviously get answers too if you can, but this is not always possible. You might see examiners' reports, intended for future candidates, which don't include answers as such but explain what common errors were made for each question and problems with scripts as a whole. Sadly these reports tend to be similar year after year, as the same errors are made. You can guess what these are – for example,

  - poor time allocation;
  - not answering all the parts of a question;
  - not answering the question as set;
  - not showing workings for a numerical answer.

- Obtain questions for practice, with answers, ideally from a variety of sources. Textbooks are the most likely source but check first (try the introduction) whether all questions have answers included in the book – it's frustrating to toil through a long answer only to discover you can't check your workings. Practising numerical techniques is obviously essential preparation for an exam, but it can also help you to understand theoretical points. When you have finished a calculation, look at it. How would you feel if this was a report on operations you were responsible for? If you had to make a decision based on this calculation, how confident would you feel?

- Read brief real-life case studies in accountancy magazines – as many as you can. These will give you a context for understanding explanations of the purpose and effect of accounting techniques in your textbooks.
- Be *active* in your revision. It is all too easy to give yourself the impression that you are working hard when reading – but is it really going in? The only way to find out is to stop – frequently – and write down key points, or do a numerical example.
- Be *honest* in your revision. Work at answering questions on your own – keep trying for the length of time you might have for such a question in an exam. If you do peek at the answer for guidance on how to proceed then there is evidently something else you have to learn before you can produce an independent answer in the examination. What is that something? Write it down. Do the example again another time. Do you get stuck in the same place or are you making progress?
- Repetition of numerical answers is beneficial. If you can, keep the sessions short and work often rather than spending several hours at it. Not only does this give your brain the chance to consolidate what you are learning and link it with other topics, but it reduces the frustration you feel when progress seems slow.
- Rather than struggle with one topic for hours on end, switch topics frequently.
- Question 'spotting' from past papers is very dangerous if this means gambling on some topics not turning up at all. You might be stronger in some areas than others, but don't leave blind spots.
- Practise neatness. This doesn't necessarily mean better handwriting (markers bless childish handwriting – it's easier to read!) – but it does mean clear numbers, straighter columns of figures, lined-up decimal points and full column headings. Where there are just a few figures which represent the final answer make them stand out – not necessarily with a rainbow of highlighter, but at least leave a blank line before and after.
- Sometimes the hardest part of writing an exam which involves numbers is matching the question with calculations you are familiar with, and then laying out an answer without time-consuming false starts, especially if a tabular format is required. You can help yourself by learning the layout of calculations. What are the labels for the columns and the main totals? Exactly what does the final result look like – should there be a £ sign or a % sign? When comparing numbers, are you looking for the highest result, or the lowest?
- Check what types of calculator are allowed in the exam. Buy a spare in good time, become familiar with it, and take both to your exam desk with you. Check batteries beforehand (and don't rely on sitting by a window to power a solar calculator!).

5

tips on interpreting essay and exam questions

This section will show you how to address exam and essay questions:

- Focus on the issues that are relevant and central.
- Read questions carefully and take account of all the words.
- Produce a balanced critique in your outline structures.
- Screen for the key words that will shape your response.
- Focus on different shades of meaning between 'discuss', 'critique', 'compare and contrast' and 'evaluate'.

What do you see?

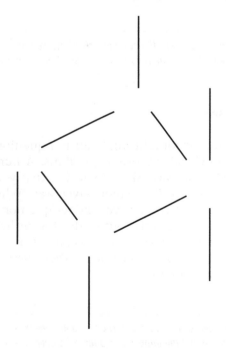

The suggested explanation for visual illusions is the inappropriate use of cues – we try to interpret three-dimensional figures in the real world with the limitations of a two dimensional screen (the retina in the eye). We use cues such as shade, texture, size, background, and so on to interpret distance, motion, shape, and so on, and we sometimes use these inappropriately. Another visual practice we engage in is to 'fill in the blanks' or join up the lines (as in the case of the nine lines above – which we might assume to be a chair). Our tendency is to impose the nearest similar and familiar template on that which we think we see. The same occurs in the social world – when we are introduced to someone of a different race we may (wrongly) assume certain things about them. The same can also apply to the way you read exam or essay questions. In these cases you are required to 'fill in the blanks' but what you fill in may be the wrong interpretation of the question. This is especially likely if you have primed yourself to expect certain questions to appear in an exam, but it can also happen in coursework essays. Although examiners do not deliberately design questions to trick you or trip you up, they cannot always prevent you from seeing things that were not designed to be there. When one student was asked what the four seasons are, the response given was, 'salt, pepper, mustard and vinegar'. This was not quite what the examiner had in mind!

> Go into the exam room, or address the coursework essay, well prepared, but be flexible enough to structure your learnt material around the slant of the question.

A politician's answer

Politicians are renowned for refusing to answer questions directly or for evading them through raising other questions. A humorous example is that when a politician was asked, 'Is it true that you always answer questions by asking another?', the reply given was, 'Who told you that?' Therefore, make sure that you answer the set question, although there may be other questions that arise out of this for further study that you might want to highlight in your conclusion. As a first principle you must answer the set question and not another question that you had hoped for in the exam or essay.

> Do not leave the examiner feeling like the person who interviews a politician and goes away with the impression that the important issues have been sidestepped.

EXAMPLE   Discuss the strategies for improving the sale of fresh fruit and vegetables in the market place at the point of delivery to the customer

Directly relevant points

- Stall and fruit kept clean.
- Well presented/arranged produce.
- Use of colour and variety.
- Position of stall in market (e.g. smells).
- Use of free samples.
- Appearance and manner of assistants.
- Competitive prices.

Less relevant points

- Advantages of organic growth.
- Arguments for vegetarianism.
- Cheaper transport for produce.
- Value of locally grown produce.
- Strategies for pest control in growth.
- Arguments for refrigeration in transit.
- Cheaper rents for markets.

Although some of the points in the second list may be relevant to sales overall, they are not as directly relevant to sales 'in the market place at the point of delivery to the customer'. If the question had included the quality of the produce then some of those issues should be addressed. Also it could be argued that some of these issues could be highlighted on a board at the stall – for example, 'only organically grown produce is sold at this stall'. So some of the points could be mentioned briefly in this way without going off on a tangent.

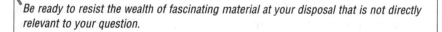

Be ready to resist the wealth of fascinating material at your disposal that is not directly relevant to your question.

Missing your question

A student bitterly complained after an exam that the topic he had revised so thoroughly had not been tested in the exam. The first response to that is that students should always cover enough topics to avoid selling themselves short in the exam – the habit of 'question spotting' is always a risky game to play. However, the reality in the anecdotal example was that the question the student was looking for was there, but he had not seen it. He had expected the question to be couched in certain words and he could not find these when he scanned over the questions in blind panic. Therefore, the simple lesson is always read over the questions carefully, slowly and thoughtfully. This practice is time well spent.

> *You can miss the question if you restrict yourself to looking for a set form of words and if you do not read over all the words carefully.*

Write it down

If you write down the question you have chosen to address, and perhaps quietly articulate it with your lips, you are more likely to process fully its true meaning and intent. Think of how easy it is to misunderstand a question that had been put to you verbally because you have misinterpreted the tone or emphasis.

> *If you read over the question several times you should be aware of all the key words and will begin to sense the connections between the ideas, and will envisage the possible directions you should take in your response.*

Take the following humorous example:

1 What is that on the road ahead?

2 What is that on the road, a head?

Question 1 calls for the identification of an object (What is that?), but question 2 has converted this into an object that suggests there has been a decapitation! Ensure therefore that you understand the direction the question is pointing you towards so that you do not go off at a tangent. One word in the question that is not properly attended to can throw you completely off track as in the following example:

1 Discuss whether the love of money is the root of all evil.

2 Discuss whether money is the root of all evil.

These are two completely different questions as 1 suggests that the real problem with money is inherent in faulty human use – that is, money itself may not be a bad thing if it is used as a servant and not a master. Whereas 2 may suggest that behind every evil act that has ever been committed money is likely to have been implicated somewhere in the motive.

Pursue a critical approach

In degree courses you are usually expected to write critically rather than merely descriptively, although it may be necessary to use some minimal descriptive substance as the raw material for your debate.

EXAMPLE Evaluate the evidence whether the American astronauts really walked on the moon, or whether this was a stage-managed hoax in a studio

Arguments for studio

- Flag blowing on moon?
- Explain the shadows.
- Why no stars seen?
- Why little dust blowing at landing?
- Can humans survive passing through the radiation belt?

Arguments for walking

- Communicates with laser reflectors left on moon.
- Retrieved rocks show patterns that are not earthly.
- How could such a hoax be protected?
- American activities were monitored by Soviets.
- Plausible explanations for arguments against walking.

Given that the question is about a critical evaluation of the evidence, you would need to address the issues one by one from both standpoints. What you should not do is digress into a tangent about the physical characteristics of the space ship or the astronauts' suits. Neither should you be drawn into a lengthy description of lunar features and contours even if you have in-depth knowledge of these.

Analyse the parts

In an effective sports team the end product is always greater than the sum of the parts. Similarly, a good essay cannot be constructed without reference to the parts. Furthermore, the parts will arise as you break down the question into the components it suggests to you. Although the breaking down of a question into components is not sufficient for an excellent essay, it is a necessary starting point.

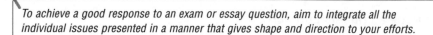

To achieve a good response to an exam or essay question, aim to integrate all the individual issues presented in a manner that gives shape and direction to your efforts.

EXAMPLE 1 Discuss whether the preservation and restoration of listed buildings is justified

Two parts to this question are clearly suggested – preservation and restoration, and you would need to do justice to each in your answer. Other issues that arise in relation to these are left for you to suggest and discuss. Examples might be finance, prioritisation, poverty, beauty, culture, modernisation, heritage and tourism.

EXAMPLE 2 Evaluate the advantages and disadvantages of giving students course credit for participation in experiments

This is a straightforward question in that you have two major sections – advantages and disadvantages. You are left with the choice of the issues that you wish to address, and you can arrange these in the order you prefer. Your aim should be to ensure that you do not have a lopsided view of this even if you feel quite strongly one way or the other.

EXAMPLE 3 Trace in a critical manner western society's changing attitudes to the corporal punishment of children

In this case you might want to consider the role of governments, religion, schools, parents and the media. However, you will need to have some reference points to the past as you are asked to address the issue of change. There would also be scope to look at where the strongest influences for change arise and where the strongest resistance comes from. You might argue that the changes have been dramatic or evolutionary.

Give yourself plenty of practice at thinking of questions in this kind of way – both with topics on and not on your course. Topics not on your course that really interest you may be a helpful way to 'break you in' to this critical way of thinking.

When asked to discuss

Students often ask how much of their own opinion they should include in an essay. In a discussion, when you raise one issue, another one can arise out of it. One tutor used to introduce his lectures by saying that he was going to 'unpack' the arguments. When you unpack an object (such as a new desk that has to be assembled), you first remove the overall packaging, such as a large box, and then proceed to remove the covers from all the component parts. After that you attempt to assemble all the parts, according to the given design, so that they hold together in the intended manner. In a discussion your aim should be not just to identify and define all the parts that contribute, but also to show where they fit into the overall picture. Your choice of components, and the way you assemble them, is unique to you – in a way, the whole essay is your 'opinion'.

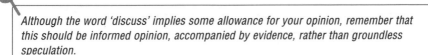

Although the word 'discuss' implies some allowance for your opinion, remember that this should be informed opinion, accompanied by evidence, rather than groundless speculation.

Checklist: Features of a response to a 'discuss' question

✓ The issues should form a chain that lead into each other in sequence.
✓ A clear shape and direction should unfold in the progression of the argument.
✓ The response should be underpinned by reference to findings and certainties.
✓ There should be identification of issues where doubt remains.
✓ The tone of argument may be tentative but should not be vague.

If a critique is requested

One example that might help clarify what is involved in a critique is the hotly debated topic of the physical punishment of children. It would be important in the interest of balance and fairness to present all sides and shades of the argument. You would then look at whether there is available evidence to support each argument, and you might introduce issues that have been coloured by prejudice, tradition, religion and legislation. It would be an aim to identify emotional arguments, arguments based on intuition and to get down to those arguments that really have solid evidence based support. Finally you would want to flag up where the strongest evidence appears to lie, and you should also identify issues that appear to be inconclusive. It would be expected that you should, if possible, arrive at some certainties.

If asked to compare and contrast

When asked to compare and contrast, you should be thinking in terms of similarities and differences. You should ask what the two issues share in common, and what features of each are distinct. Your preferred strategy for tackling this might be to work first through all the similarities and then through all the contrasts (or vice versa). On the other hand, work through a similarity and contrast, followed by another similarity and contrast, etc.

EXAMPLE   **Compare and contrast the uses of tea and coffee as beverages**

Similarities

- Usually drunk hot.
- Can be drunk without food.
- Can be taken with a snack or meal.
- Can be drunk with milk.
- Can be taken with honey, sugar or sweeteners.
- Both contain caffeine.
- Both can be addictive.

Contrasts

- Differences in taste.
- Tea perhaps preferred at night.
- Differences in caffeine content.
- Coffee more bitter.
- Coffee sometimes taken with cream or whisky.
- Each perhaps preferred with different foods.
- Coffee preferred for hangover.

When you compare and contrast you should aim to paint a true picture of the full 'landscape'.

Whenever evaluation is requested

EXAMPLE   TV soap opera director

Imagine that you are a TV director for a popular soap opera which has been broadcast for 10 years. In recent months that you have lost some viewers to an alternative soap opera on a rival channel, which has used some fresh ideas and new actors and has a big novelty appeal. It will take time to see if their level of viewing can be sustained, but you run the risk that you might lose some more viewers at least in the short term. You have been given the task of evaluating the programme to see if you can ascertain why you have retained the faithful but lost other viewers, and what you could do to improve the programme without compromising the aspects that work.

In your task you might want to review past features (retrospective), outline present features (perspective) and envisage positive future changes (prospective).

This illustration may provoke you to think about how you might approach a question that asks you to evaluate some theory or concept. Some summary points are presented below:

- Has the theory/concept stood the test of time?
- Is there a supportive evidence base that would not easily be overturned?
- Are there questionable elements that have been or should be challenged?
- Does more recent evidence point to a need for modification?
- Is the theory/concept robust and likely to be around for the foreseeable future?
- Could it be strengthened through being merged with other theories/concepts?

It should be noted that the words presented in the above examples might not always be the exact words that will appear on your exam script – for example, you might find 'analyse', or 'outline', or 'investigate', and so on. The best advice is to check over your past exam papers and familiarise yourself with the words that are most recurrent.

In summary, this section has been designed to give you reference points to measure where you are at in your studies, and to help you map out the way ahead in manageable increments. It should now be clear that learning should not merely be a mechanical exercise, such as just memorising and reproducing study material. Good quality learning also involves making connections between ideas, thinking at a deeper level by attempting to understand your material and developing a critical approach to learning.

However, this cannot be achieved without the discipline of preparation for lectures, seminars and exams, or without learning to structure your material (headings and subheadings) and to set each unit of learning within its overall context in your subject and programme. It is also vital to keep your subject materials in organised folders so that you can add/extract/replace materials when you need to. An important device in learning is to develop the ability to ask questions (whether written, spoken or silent). Another useful device in learning is to illustrate your material and use examples that will help make your study fun, memorable and vivid. It is useful to set problems for yourself that will allow you to think through solutions and therefore enhance the quality of your learning.

Your aim should be to become an 'all round student' who engages in and benefits from all the learning activities available to you (lectures, seminars, tutorials, computing, laboratories, discussions, library work, and so on), and to develop all the academic and personal skills that will put you in the driving seat to academic achievement. It will be motivating and confidence building for you if you can recognise the value of these qualities, both across your academic programme and beyond graduation to the world of work. They will also serve you well in your continued commitment to life long learning.

Further reading

McIlroy, D. (2003) *Studying at University: How to be a Successful Student.* London. SAGE.

6	
exam tips	

This section will show you how to:

- Develop strategies for controlling your nervous energy.
- Manage time in exams.
- Attend to the practical details associated with the exam.
- Stay focused on the exam questions.
- Link revision outlines to strategy for addressing exam questions.
- Tackle numerical answers in exams.

Handling your nerves

Exam nerves are not unusual and it has been concluded that test anxiety arises because of the perception that your performance is being evaluated, that the consequences are likely to be serious and that you are working under the pressure of a time restriction.

Activities that may help reduce or buffer the effects of exam stress:

- Listening to music.
- Going for a brisk walk.
- Simple breathing exercises.
- Some muscle relaxation.
- Watching a movie.
- Enjoying some laughter.
- Doing some exercise.
- Relaxing in a bath (with music if preferred).

Time management in the exam

The all-important matter as you approach an exam is to develop the belief that you can take control over the situation. As you work through the list of issues that you need to address, you will be able to tick them off one by one. One of the issues you will need to be clear about *before* the exam is the length of time you should allocate to each question. Sometimes this can be quite simple (although it is always necessary to read the rubric carefully) – for example, if two questions are to be answered in a two hour paper, you should allow one hour for each question. If it is a two hour paper with one essay question and five shorter answers, you could allow one hour for the essay and 12 minutes each for the shorter questions. However, you always need to check out the exact marks allowed for each question, and you will also need to deduct whatever time it takes you to read over the paper and to choose your questions. See if you can work out a time management strategy in each of the following scenarios. More importantly, give yourself some practice on the papers you are likely to face.

Remember to check if the structure of your exam paper is the same as in previous years, and remember that excessive time on your 'strongest' question will not compensate for very poor answers to other questions. Also ensure that you read the rubric carefully in the exam.

Examples for working out the division of exam labour by time.

1   A three hour paper with four compulsory questions (equally weighted in marks).

2   A three hour paper with two essays and ten short questions (each of the three sections carry one third of the marks).

3   A two hour paper with two essay questions and 100 multiple choice questions (half marks are on the two essays and half marks on the multiple choice section).

Get into the calculating frame of mind and be sure to have the calculations done before the exam. Ensure that the structure of the exam has not changed since the last one. Also deduct the time taken to read over the paper in allocating time to each question.

Suggested answers to previous exercise.

1 This allows 45 minutes for each question (4 questions × 45 minutes = 3 hours). However, if you allow 40 minutes for each question this will give you 20 minutes (4 questions × 5 minutes) to read over the paper and plan your outlines.

2 In this example you can spend 1 hour on each of the two major questions, and 1 hour on the 10 short questions. For the two major questions you could allow 10 minutes for reading and planning on each, and 50 minutes for writing. In the 10 short questions, you could allow 6 minutes in total for each (10 questions × 6 minutes = 60 minutes). However, if you allow approximately 1 minute reading and planning time, this will allow 5 minutes writing time for each question.

3 In this case you have to divide 120 minutes by 3 sections – this allows 40 minutes for each. You could for example allow 5 minutes reading/planning time for each essay and 35 minutes for writing (or 10 minutes reading/planning and 30 minutes writing). After you have completed the two major questions you are left with 40 minutes to tackle the 100 multiple choice questions.

You may not be able to achieve total precision in planning time for tasks, but you will have a greater feeling of control and confidence if you have some reference points to guide you.

After you have decided on the questions you wish to address, you then need to plan your answers. Some students prefer to plan all outlines and draft work at the beginning, whilst other prefer to plan and address one answer before proceeding to address the next question. Decide on your strategy before you enter the exam room and stick to your plan.

Keep awareness of time limitations and this will help you to write succinctly, keep focused on the task and prevent you dressing up your responses with unnecessary padding.

Some students put as much effort into their rough work as they do into their exam essay.

Checklist: Practical exam details

✓ Check that you have the correct venue and time.
✓ Make sure you know how to get to the venue before the exam day.
✓ Allow sufficient time for your journey and consider the possibility of delays.
✓ Bring *extra* pens, calculator, etc.
✓ Take a small bottle of water if allowed; also tissues, mints, etc.
✓ Put your vital possessions in a (small, strong, see-through, quiet) plastic bag – you may not be allowed to take large bags to your desk with you. Pack the plastic bag the night before and check the contents again in the morning.
✓ Remember your watch, and any required identification documents or cards.
✓ Fill in required personal details before the exam begins if allowed.

Control wandering thoughts

Try to concentrate all the way through the exam – easier said than done. Distracting thoughts may be a form of escape from the stressful situation. Lecturing yourself won't help. Instead try switching tasks – from planning to writing finished work or vice versa. Or turn your attention to physical matters for a moment – exercise your hands or rotate your ankles or shoulders. Mints are good too.

Links to revision

If you have followed the guidelines given for revision, you will be well equipped with outline plans when you enter the exam room. You may have chosen to use headings and subheadings, mind maps, hierarchical approaches or just a series of simple mnemonics. Whatever method you choose to use, you should be furnished with a series of memory triggers that will open the treasure house door for you once you begin to write.

> Although you may have clear templates with a definite structure or framework for organising your material, you will need to be flexible about how this should be applied to your exam questions. Unless the question says 'Write all you know about … ' (very unlikely) you need to tailor your answer for the specific question posed.

The art of 'name dropping'

In most topics at university you will be required to cite studies as evidence for your arguments and to link these to the names of researchers, scholars or theorists. It will help if you can use the correct dates or at least the decades, and it is good to demonstrate that you have used contemporary sources, and have done some independent work. An assessor will have dozens if not hundreds of scripts to work through and they will know if you are just repeating the same phrases from the same sources as every one else. There is inevitably a certain amount of this that must go on, but there is room for you to add fresh and original touches that demonstrate independence and imagination.

> As well as citing sources, you can impress the examiner by citing up-to-date examples of what you are discussing. Make it your business to locate some suitable examples as you revise.

In the management accounting examination ...

- In numerical answers method is more important than accuracy. You will get marks for correct technique even if your arithmetic fails you. So make sure all your workings are in plain view – this is the only way the assessor can check the method you used. This is extremely important – in fact a perfectly correct answer with no visible workings might not even get full marks. If you really want to make private jottings, and you are writing in a stapled answer booklet, use the last page in the booklet.
- The first 50% of marks are a lot easier than the remaining 50%, even for numerical answers – in other words only spend time perfecting your answer if you are absolutely sure you can afford the time.
- Maybe you know you routinely have a problem with time management in exams. Once you have decided which questions you will answer, make a little table for yourself, showing not only how long you will have for each question, but also at what time you should be starting each one.
- If the question is divided into parts, this is the basis for the marking scheme. Try to spend the right amount of time on each part of the question according to the marks allocated. It's tempting to focus on the numerical part of the question and hurry over, or even overlook, a requirement for an explanation or discussion worth perhaps 5 or 10 marks: but your work will be marked according to the part marks, so don't throw marks away.
- Label things clearly – columns, totals, axes of graphs.
- Try to have a rough idea of the correct answer so that if you make a slip with your calculator you have a chance of spotting it.
- If the rubric asks you to start each question on a new page (or even if it doesn't), do exactly that, and write the *correct* question number at the top of the page. Within the question, label each part clearly in the left margin. Write as clearly as you can – and use black pen or at least a very dark blue, if you must use blue. Spread out – you didn't buy the paper – for clarity, and to leave space for alterations or additions if necessary. Leave a blank line after each paragraph. Leave a blank line (or two) before each total in tables of figures for the same reasons.
- Spare a thought for the poor assessor, toiling over a pile of exam scripts. If there is a section on the front of the answer booklet for the numbers of the questions you chose, complete this as you go along, making sure the numbers appear in the same order as they appear in the booklet. That's what this section is for – to help the assessor find specific answers, since they may be working through the pile of scripts one question at a time. Just write the question number once, even if there are several parts to the question (write '2', not 2a, 2b, etc.).
- Try to believe this: the assessor *wants* you to do well. The marking process is essentially one of searching each script for items to reward. This is not an exact science or a mechanical process, alas. What the assessor is doing is trying to find evidence that the candidate understands a calculation or issue. Make that process as easy as possible. Good luck!

glossary

ABC	See **activity-based costing**.
Absorption costing	A variant of **standard costing** which includes indirect manufacturing costs.
Accounting rate of return	A method of investment appraisal based on standard methods of accounting.
Activity-based costing	A variation of standard costing which attempts to allocate costs more accurately, particularly where production runs vary in volume.
ARR	See **accounting rate of return**.
Break-even point	The volume of sales at which there is neither profit nor loss.
Budget	A quantified business plan.
Cash budget	The part of a budget that deals with cash flows and balances.
Contribution	The excess of sales revenues over variable costs, which may be regarded as a contribution to fixed costs and profit.
Cost-plus	A method of pricing by reference to cost.

Cost-volume-profit analysis	Analysis of cost and profit within a small range of production (the **relevant range**), often using graphs.
CVP analysis	See **cost-volume-profit analysis**.
Decision tree	A graphical method for dealing with decisions.
Depreciation	A charge which spreads the cost of fixed assets over their useful life.
Direct costs	Costs which can be allocated to a particular item.
Direct labour	Costs of employees who work on producing goods.
Direct materials	Costs of materials used in production.
Discount rate	The rate at which cash flows are discounted to give **net present value**.
Economic order quantity	The size of order that minimises costs.
Efficiency variance	**Variance** in the amount of labour hours used.
EOQ	See **economic order quantity**.
Estimating	The process of generating a cost and quotation for a new product.
Fixed costs	Costs which do not vary with the level of output.
Flexed budget	A budget wherein projected costs have been adjusted appropriately for an excess or deficit in production.
Indirect costs	Costs which cannot be allocated to a particular item.

Indirect labour   Costs of employees who do not work on producing goods, e.g. administrators, sales-people, accountants.

Indirect materials   Costs of materials not used in production, e.g. packaging, stationery.

Internal rate of return   The discount rate that gives a **net present value** of zero to a stream of receipts and payments.

Inventory   See **stock**.

IRR   See **internal rate of return**.

Irrelevant costs   Costs which should be ignored for a calculation or decision.

Job costing   A method used for discrete jobs which are quoted for individually.

Limiting factor   A factor of production (e.g. material, machine time, skilled labour) which limits production capacity.

Linear programming   A method of optimising **product mix** where there is more than one **limiting factor**.

Loss   The difference between revenues and related costs, if negative. If positive, the difference is a **profit**.

Margin of safety   The number of units sold in excess of the **break-even point**.

Marginal cost   The cost of making one additional unit of output.

MRP   Materials requirement planning, often used to refer to software for that purpose.

Net present value	The value of a stream of cash flows discounted at an appropriate rate to equate to the equivalent of a single lump sum paid or received at the present date.
NPV	See **net present value**.
Operating cycle	The length of time from receipt of raw materials to receipt of payment for finished goods from customer.
Opportunity cost	Profit or revenue forgone as a consequence of a decision.
Overheads	Fixed indirect costs, perhaps from the idea that the roof over one's head must be paid for even if no production takes place.
Payback	A method of investment appraisal based on the time taken for income to exceed outlay.
Present value	The value of a future payment or receipt discounted at an appropriate rate to equate to a current value.
Price variance	**Variance** in the price of materials or other non-labour resources.
Process costing	A method applied to production of goods resulting from a series of processes.
Product mix	The volumes of different goods produced.
Profit	The difference between revenues and related costs, if positive. If negative, the difference is a **loss**.
PV	See **present value**.
Rate variance	**Variance** in the labour rate.

Relevant costs	Costs which should be taken into account for a calculation or decision.
Relevant range	The range of output within which calculations are valid.
Return on investment	The profit on an investment expressed as a percentage of the amount invested.
ROI	See **return on investment**.
Sales mix	The volumes of different goods sold.
Sales mix variance	**Variance** arising from sales of different products in different proportions from the budget.
Set-up time	The time taken to make a production line ready for a new product.
Simplex algorithm	A standard method for solving linear programming equations.
Standard costing	A system of costing based on establishing standard values for resources used for the production of a single item.
Stock	Materials held for resale. Raw materials are in the state in which they were purchased; finished goods are completed and ready for sale; work-in-progress is in an intermediate state where some work has been done on the materials but there is more to do.
Sub-contracting	Commissioning an external contractor to carry out some aspect of production.
Sunk costs	Costs which have been incurred or contracted for and cannot be recovered by any current or future action.

Transfer pricing	The issues related to the prices at which transactions are carried out within segments of the same company or group.
Usage variance	**Variance** in the amount of material or other non-labour resources used.
Value-added tax	A tax on goods and services which affects the cash-flow, not the profits, of VAT-registered bodies.
Variable costs	Costs which vary with the level of output.
Variance	The difference between expected and actual outcomes in a standard costing system. Variances are either favourable or adverse.
VAT	See **value-added tax**.
WACC	See **weighted average cost of capital**.
Weighted average cost of capital	The average cost of a company's capital weighted according to market value.
Zero-based budgeting	A budget process which assumes a starting level of zero for all expenses, rather than some other point such as last year's outcome.

references

Atrill P. and McLaney E. (2005) *Management Accounting for Decision Makers, 4th edition.* Englewood Cliffs, NJ: Prentice Hall.

Coombs, H., Hobbs, D. and Jenkins, E. (2005) *Management Accounting.* London: Sage.

Drury, C. (2004) *Management and Cost Accounting, 6th edition.* London: Thomson Learning.

Horngren, C., Sundem, G. and Stratton, W. (2004) *Introduction to Management Accounting, 13th edition.* Harlow: Pearson.

Upchurch, A. (2003) *Management Accounting Principles and Practice.* Englewood Cliffs, NJ: Prentice Hall.

Weetman, P. (2002) *Financial and Management Accounting: An Introduction, 3rd edition.* Harlow: Pearson.

index